The Miracle of the
HOLY HOUSE
OF LORETO

FEDERICO CATANI, born in Jesi (Ancona), Italy, in 1986, graduated with a degree in Political Science at LUISS - Free International University of Social Studies, "Guido Carli" (Rome) and Religious Sciences at the Pontifical University of the Holy Cross (Rome). He served as a Catholic religion teacher in state schools. A journalist and publicist, he writes for various magazines and blogs in the Catholic world. He is the director of *Spunti*, of the *Luci Sull'Est* Association.

*I express my gratitude to Father **Giuseppe Santarelli** and Sister Luigia Busani, who kindly opened to me the doors of the Loreto Archive-Museum.*

I also thank Prof. Giorgio Nicolini for his valuable advice and information.

*A special thanks to Mr. **Nestor Fonseca** for his material and spiritual help, without which this book would not have been possible.*

To order more copies of this book, contact:

U.S.A.
America Needs Fatima
(888) 317-5571
P.O. Box 341, Hanover, PA 17331
ANF@ANF.org · www.ANF.org

Canada
Canada Needs Our Lady
P.O. Box 36040, Greenfield Park, QC   J4V 3N7
1-844-729-6279 (1-844-Say-Mary)
www.CanadaNeedsOurLady.org
Info@CanadaNeedsOurLady.org

Cover: Translation of the Holy House. Francesco Foschi, eighteenth century. Ancient Treasure Museum of the Holy House, Loreto.

Photographs and graphic design: Felipe Barandiarán

English translation: José A. Schelini

© 2020 English translation:
The Foundation for a Christian Civilization, Inc.
1358 Jefferson Road, Spring Grove, PA 17362

Library of Congress Control Number: 2021930177
ISBN: 978-1-877905-62-9

Printed in the United States of America.

Federico Catani

The Miracle of the
HOLY HOUSE
OF LORETO

AMERICA NEEDS FATIMA
(888) 317-5571
www.ANF.org – ANF@ANF.org

I offer this work as a sign of gratitude to Our Lady, and above all, mindful of her recommendation at Fatima, in reparation for the sins committed against her privileges.

The Annunciation. Federico Barocci, chapel of the Dukes of Urbino, Basilica of Loreto

"At that time, the angel Gabriel was sent by God into a city of Galilee, called Nazareth, to a virgin espoused to a man whose name was Joseph, of the house of David; and the virgin's name was Mary. And the angel having come in, said unto her: 'Hail, full of grace, the Lord is with thee: blessed art thou among women.'

Having heard that, she was troubled at his saying, and thought to herself what manner of salutation this should be. And the angel said to her: 'Fear not, Mary, for thou hast found grace with God. Behold thou shalt conceive in thy womb, and shalt bring forth a son; and thou shalt call his name Jesus. He shall be great, and shall be called the Son of the most High; and the Lord God shall give unto him the throne of David his father; and he shall reign in the house of Jacob forever. And of his kingdom there shall be no end.'

And Mary said to the angel: 'How shall this be done, because I know not man?' And the angel answering, said to her: 'The Holy Ghost shall come upon thee, and the power of the most High shall overshadow thee. And therefore also the Holy One which shall be born of thee shall be called the Son of God. And behold thy cousin Elizabeth, she also hath conceived a son in her old age; and this is the sixth month for her that is called barren: Because nothing shall be impossible with God.'

And Mary said: 'Behold the handmaid of the Lord; be it done to me according to thy word.' And the angel departed from her."

(Gospel of St. Luke, 1:26-38)

CONTENTS

It All Started Here...

On August 15, 1993, in a letter sent on the occasion of the seventh centenary of the Shrine of the Holy House of Loreto, Pope John Paul II called it "the first international sanctuary dedicated to the Virgin and, for several centuries, the true Marian heart of Christianity."

In fact, Loreto is a temple unlike many others. And not only because it has long been the most important center of Marian devotion in Italy and Europe, but above all for the precious relic it houses, and for how it arrived in the Marche region of Italy.

As Saint Bernard mentioned in a splendid homily, the Holy House of Loreto is the place where the Redemption of humanity began.[1] It is the very humble cell in which the most important event of history took place: the Annunciation of the Blessed Virgin Mary and the consequent Incarnation of the Divine Word. Among

---

1   You have heard, Virgin, that you will conceive and give birth to a son; you have heard that this will not happen by the work of man but by that of the Holy Spirit. The angel awaits your answer; he must take it back to God who sent him. We too, O Lady, are waiting for a word of compassion, we miserably oppressed by a sentence of damnation. Behold the price of our salvation is offered to you: if you consent, we will be immediately freed. We were all created by the eternal Word of God but are now subject to death: By your short answer, must we be renewed and brought back to life. O pious Virgin, Adam, exiled from heaven with his miserable descent, begs this of you in tears; Abraham and David, the holy patriarchs, your ancestors also living in the shadowy region of death, urgently plead with you to accept. The whole world awaits prostrated at your knees: From your mouth depends the consolation of the poor, the redemption of prisoners, the liberation of the condemned, the salvation of all the children of Adam, of all mankind" (Cf. *Omelie sulla Madonna* of Saint Bernard, Abbot, Hom. 4, 8-9; *Opera omnia*, ed. Cisterc. 4, 1966, 53-54). (Our translation.)

the walls that were once in Nazareth, a remote and miserable village in northern Palestine, God became a man to save humanity from sin; the Eternal came into time to restore the universe wounded by the original guilt. It all happened thanks to the cooperation of a woman who, with her "Yes," her *"Fiat,"* changed the course of events forever by contributing in her own and very special way, as Co-Redemptrix, to the redemption of the world.

The Holy Family in the House of Nazareth.
Fresco by Modesto Faustini

That poor dwelling, in which the immaculate conception and birth of Mary Most Holy took place, belonged to her parents, Saints Joachim and Anna. The Ever-Virgin and her spouse Saint Joseph chose it as their common home precisely because of the sanctity that it emanated and because the Incarnation took place there. The Holy Family lived and grew in that house, and Jesus was raised and worked there until the beginning of his public life.

Daily, and for many years, the walls which are now in Loreto saw the holy faces of Jesus, Mary and Joseph, listened to their voices, breaths and prayers, were touched by their hands, and remained impregnated with holiness and divinity so much as to convey, already on this earth, a foretaste of Paradise. Saint Joseph died among those walls, in the arms of his Son and his most holy spouse. In that house, the Apostles celebrated the Holy Sacrifice of the Mass, where Christ became present again in the Eucharist just as years before, in the same place, he had become a man in the womb of his most holy Mother, after the announcement by the archangel Gabriel.

Italy has the extraordinary grace of hosting this hallowed relic on its territory, which according to the tradition of the Church and the endorsement of countless historical, archaeological, and scientific studies, was miraculously "translated" into the grounds of Loreto through the "ministry of the angels."

Such a portentous event deserves to be known or rediscovered. People often take for granted or fail to appreciate what they have at hand. Yet, we must never forget that nothing is due to us: the gift of the Holy House must be made to bear fruit and be used to help everyone move towards the path of holiness.

The first step to take is to know in order to better love. To know, we must draw only on certain, safe, and perfectly documented facts, events, and data. That is exactly what this work strives to do.

Chapter I

How Is the Holy House Made?

The story of Loreto begins in Nazareth, where Mary Most Holy received the angelic salutation.

In the Palestine of that time, the homes of humble people usually consisted of three walls leaning against a cave, which constituted a separate room. It is certainly not implausible that there could be other small premises and an external courtyard. However, the main room was the one leaning against the cave. This obviously also applies to the residence of the Holy Family of Nazareth, which, despite belonging to the royal lineage of David, was humble and austere (although not as miserable as certain pauperist Catholics would have us believe).

Since the origins of Christianity, as is known, the cell where the Incarnation of the Word of God took place with the "Yes" of Our Lady was turned into a place of worship and pilgrimage. In practice, it has been venerated since Mary Most Holy was still on earth.

Over time, efforts were made to render the environment more suitable to accommodate the huge influx of faithful. In fact, the chapel was gradually incorporated into a larger structure. From a synagogue church of the era of Emperor Constantine, it eventually became a basilica, first built by Byzantines, and later by Crusaders.

During this period, devout pilgrims (but also thieves and members of the clergy engaging in simony) removed some stones or fragments from those sacred walls so their custodians had to make up for it by adding

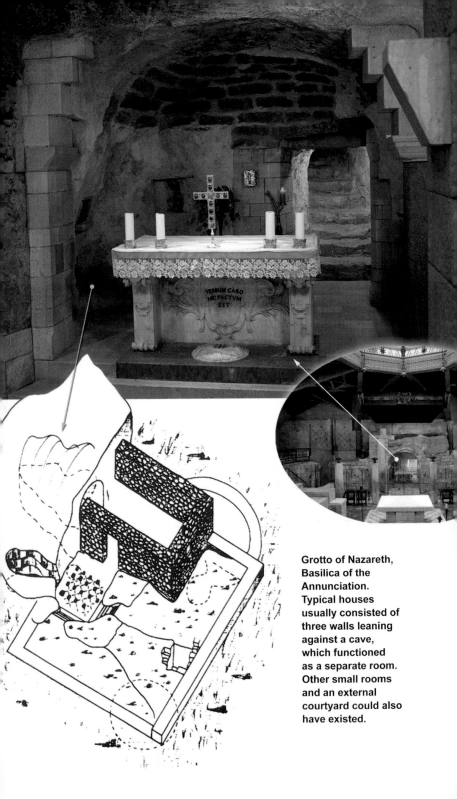

Grotto of Nazareth, Basilica of the Annunciation. Typical houses usually consisted of three walls leaning against a cave, which functioned as a separate room. Other small rooms and an external courtyard could also have existed.

new material in some places. In short, the building underwent some minor functional transformations to ensure its optimum conservation. It is also certain and undeniable that for centuries, the abode of the Ever-Virgin was preserved from all danger. The Holy House was spared even in 1263, when Islamic armies razed the Basilica of the Annunciation, under which it stood.

The presence of the Crusaders in Palestine to defend the Holy Places ended in May 1291, with the Muslim conquest of the last Christian stronghold, St. John of Acre. However, a few days before the final defeat of the Crusader army, the cell of the Blessed Mother inexplicably disappeared from Nazareth.

All the pilgrims who went there after that date confirmed that they saw only the cave but not the three walls.

1.1 But Is It Really the House of Our Lady?

Over the centuries – starting with the Protestants, and followed by the Enlightenment – many critical voices questioned the authenticity of the Holy House of Loreto. Rationalist and materialist thinkers have always tried to refute everything that appears sacred and miraculous, because they do not accept the existence of something, or rather Someone, that transcends and surpasses the earthly world. In short, they do not want to recognize the bursting in of the supernatural in history.

However, proofs of the authenticity of the Holy House of Loreto are not lacking, and most are provided by technical and scientific research.

While those who insist on not believing will always find a reason to justify their false opinion, Loreto stands before the eyes of all as a permanent miracle. Let us now go on to examine some elements that allow us to reasonably state that the walls found in perfect condition in the Loreto sanctuary are those among which the Holy Family of Nazareth lived, and which were miraculously transported to Italy.

• A building without a foundation?

Looking at the characteristics of the Holy House, one cannot but be amazed by this miracle that has lasted for over seven centuries. It is not even a question of "believing," but simply one of seeing. Therefore, it is up to the critics to prove their position.

1) While granting that from the structural point of view, studies have confirmed that the building has not undergone any substantial change over time, we must first point out a very curious fact.

The three walls of the Holy House have no foundations of their own and are placed on bare and uneven ground. They are not at the same level because part of them is suspended on the void of a ditch. This is absolutely inconceivable for any construction, however rudimentary – except for buildings like those in Palestine at the time of Jesus – that stood against a cave and thus had the living rock as their foundation. Now if a house (or a place of worship) is built from scratch, as Loreto's critics have always suggested, why would anyone build it without a foundation and protruding into a ditch?

Furthermore, during various archaeological excavations, a bush of grass was also discovered, part of it crushed by a wall of the house,[2] and the other part protruding from under the same wall, as if the walls had been lowered and supported from above, on a dusty

---

2   Cf. G. Nicolini in *Nuovi studi confermano l'autenticità della Santa Casa di Maria a Loreto*, Agenzia Internazionale Zenit, Rome March 28, 2006.

The walls are made a kind of stone and mortar that do not exist in the Marche region of Italy. Its style of construction and material are typical of the Holy Land. Graffiti of clearly Judeo-Christian origin are engraved on various stones.

Graffiti, with syncopated writing in Greek, read *Iesous Christos Theou Yios* (Jesus Christ Son of God). Two Hebrew letters (*lamed* and *waw*) can also be identified.

Graffiti representing a semi-cosmic cross, a Judeo-Christian symbol of Pleroma and Kenoma, that is, a sign of fullness and imperfection, Heaven and Earth

The three walls of the Holy House have no foundations of their own and are placed on bare, irregular, and uneven ground; they are not at the same level because part of them is suspended over the void of a ditch.

ground not cleaned by anyone before their placement. Which construction company would work like that?

Only at a later date, for fear that the relic could collapse or be damaged, the inhabitants of Recanati (in whose territory the Holy House had ultimately arrived) laid the foundations and built around its walls the so-called "recanatesi walls" (which, however, as we will see shortly, are located at a distance from the sacred walls). These interventions only demonstrate the preciousness of the building, seemingly so poor and insignificant, and beg this basic question: If it really was a human, money-making operation to make people believe it was an illustrious relic, why did they not immediately do those jobs, more demanding and expensive than simple foundations?

2) Another relevant datum. The walls are located on what, at the time of the events, was a public road in the municipality of Recanati, a place of transit on which it was forbidden to build for obvious reasons, as shown by engineer Nanni Monelli's well-documented research. Municipal regulations required the demolition of any structures built there without permission. Well, that evidently did not happen with the Holy House because of its sacredness and the miraculous way in which it had come, as the community immediately recognized.

Moreover, considering that in the thirteenth century, there were plenty of public spaces to build (both municipal and ecclesiastical property), why would the authorities have spent so many resources to open a new section of road to replace the one occupied by the Holy House? Had the entire operation of the Nazareth residence been a human work that someone decided to build and pass off as the Holy House, why would the locals not have picked a more suitable spot? It would have sufficed to place the building only 200 yards away to the west, on one of the two mounds that flanked that same road.

3) But it does not end there. As always, archaeological excavations over the centuries (the latest date back to the years 1962-1965), have directly verified that the perimeter of the Holy House of Loreto perfectly coincides with that of the ancient house of Nazareth. From its foundations, which remain to this day, the walls seem to have been torn up. Even more extraordinary and corroborating is that exactly the same perimeter is found in Trsat (Croatia), the exact place where the

Holy House remained for about three and a half years before reaching Loreto, as we will see later. Is it mere coincidence, or does this attest to its authenticity as the home of the Holy Family of Nazareth?

4) One should bear in mind that the location of the original door and window is inconceivable for a small temple built specifically in Loreto. In fact, unlike the common usage in the Marche region, the door is on the long side (and not on the short side as in all churches), and the window, positioned to the west, is inadequate to receive adequate afternoon lighting. These anomalies can only be explained if the house is relocated to its original position, in front of the cave of Nazareth.

5) In addition, it is undoubtedly very helpful to verify the material with which the Holy House is built. Its walls are made with a type of stone and mortar that do not exist in the Marche region. Its construction style and material are typical of the Holy Land. Studies have always confirmed this beyond any possible doubt. The presence of some non-original bricks introduced in the late Byzantine period is explained by the restorations or adaptations made necessary because of the huge influx of pilgrims. They, therefore, preceded the miraculous translation. The presence of cedarwood also confirms the origin from the Nazareth area near the southern hills of Lebanon, known for that type of tree.

6) Different stones have graffiti of clear Judeo-Christian origin, absolutely foreign to the environment and history of the Marche region. Evidently, early pilgrims attested to their faith with those little engravings when they devoutly visited that highly sacred place so full of meaning. Note also that some graffiti seems to be upside down, which can be explained by work that closed the original door in 1531-1535. The stones removed to make the two new openings were used to wall the old one, and masons may have accidentally inserted the stones backward.

7) Finally, let us hear from the architects who studied the Holy House.

Giuseppe Sacconi, director of the restoration of the Loreto Basilica from 1884 to 1905, noted that "the Holy House is resting in part on the edge of an old road and partly suspended above the adjoining ditch,"[3] which is why it could not have been built or rebuilt as it is in its location.

Federico Mannucci, following studies and surveys commissioned by the ecclesiastical authority, stated in a 1922 report that, "the wall of the Holy House ends a few centimeters below the floor and the ground on which it rests is dissolved." Furthermore, "in some places, the wall was found to be almost completely isolated from the ground below." Therefore, in a letter he sent that same year to the then-bishop of Loreto and Recanati, Most Rev. Alfonso Maria Andreoli, Mannucci came to these conclusions: "The walls of the Holy House, although of rough appearance, are perfectly constructed with horizontal rows of stone. They necessarily require a foundation that ensures solid support or at least a preparation of the ground to make possible its special structure in horizontal layers. However, the walls of the Holy House have no foundation or preparation whatsoever in the ground below, which is completely loose and dusty. Therefore, one can conclude with certainty that the construction of the Holy House could not have taken place where it is found.

---

3   Cit. in G. Nicolini, "Alcune 'prove' storiche, archeologiche e scientifiche comprovanti 'la verità' delle miracolose traslazioni della Santa Casa di Nazareth a Loreto", in *Il segno del soprannaturale* no. 210, December 2005, p. 18.

"... It is absurd to think that the shrine could have been transported by mechanical means; its prodigious translation, therefore, remains fully confirmed, as is evidenced by historical documents, the centuries-old tradition, and the uninterrupted consensus of the Church. I conclude by pointing out that it is surprising and extraordinary that the building of the Holy House, although having no foundation, is situated on a ground that offers no support, being loose and overloaded, albeit partially, with the weight of the vault built in place of the roof. Yet the ground remains unaltered, without caving in at all or causing the slightest crack in the walls.[4]

No one has ever been able to disprove these data, fully confirmed by the excavations of 1962-1965.

• A few of the countless miraculous events

Since the walls of the Holy House rested directly on the ground without foundations, for fear they would collapse, the Recanatesians placed sub-foundations and surrounded them with a retaining wall, the so-called "wall of the Recanati." However, an exceptional event took place: at the end of the work, the newly-built wall broke away from the sacred walls so much so that — as Father Raffaele Riera[5] recounts — a child could easily pass through them and show people the truth of the miracle with the help of a lit candle. This phenomenon was also noted by the architect Rainero Nerucci during the construction of the imposing marble cladding, in the times of Pope Clement VII. Even today, the distance between this wall and the sacred walls is 4.4 inches. In this way,

---

4   Cit. in G. Gorel, *La santa Casa di Loreto*, Edizioni Paoline, Catania 1962, pp. 116 & ff.

5   Father Raffaele Riera, Jesuit and penitentiary at Loreto from 1554 to 1582, author of *Historia Domus Lauretanae Liber singularis* (circa 1565). Cf. G. Santarelli, *La Santa Casa di Loreto*, cit., p. 16.

The marble cladding of the Holy House. Designed by Donato Braman-te, commissioned by Pope Julius II, Pope Leo X entrusted the work to Andrea Sansovino, who was succeeded by Raniero Nerucci and Antonio da Sangallo the Younger.

the Holy Virgin seems to want to show that she does not need human help to keep her home standing.[6]

Then there is the question of openings in the Holy House. Originally, the only point where you could enter or leave was in the middle of the north-ern wall, in front of which was the altar (later moved to the eastern part). However, problems arose due to the huge numbers of pilgrims who devotedly visited the sacred relic. In the sixteenth century, the popes

6   Cf. G. Gorel, *La santa Casa di Loreto*, cit., p. 100.

Julius II and Leo X established that the old door had to be closed to open two more to facilitate the pilgrims' exit. At the time of Pope Clement VII, the faithful protested against what they saw as a profanation, so they decided to do the work at night. Here is how Riera, mentioned above, describes the facts:

"The architect [Rainero Nerucci], accompanied by some selected workers, entered the Holy House to carry out the orders received. With a pointer, the architect draws on the wall the dimensions of the doors to be opened and strongly strikes the wall with a hammer, telling his men: 'Break through here and open the door.' But at this very moment, his arm is seized by a strong tremor; he pales, his whole body goes limp and, feeling as if he was dying, he retracts the order. He is brought home almost lifeless and laid on his bed, where he remains unconscious for eight hours. When he comes to, he prays to the Virgin of Loreto, who soon helps him. Clement VII, moved to tears, consults heaven again before proceeding. Illuminated from above, he repeats his order: "*Muros sacri sacelli* – he wrote to the architect – *non timeas aperire portasque conficere, sic jubet Clemens Septimus.*"[7]

At the same time, the pope advised him to arm himself not only with chisel and hammer, but also with prayer and fasting. Nerucci, still shaken with emotion, refused to obey the pontiff's orders, and the work remained suspended until a young priest of the basilica, after three days of fasting and prayers, offered to replace him. Entering the Holy House and surrounded by clergy and faithful, he publicly proclaimed the purity of his intentions: "O Holy Virgin, I am not the one who will

---

7   "Do not be afraid to open the walls of the sacred shrine and make doors, orders Clement the Seventh."

strike the walls of your dwelling with this hammer: it is Clement, the Vicar of Your Son, and he has given this order for your greater glory." Having said that prayer, he advanced, struck the first blow, then a second, and the stones came off almost by themselves. In this way, the doors were opened, and the center of the northern wall was closed with part of the materials. One can still see the cedar frame and lintel."[8]

Because of these episodes, since Our Lady had shown herself rather jealous of her home, the Church has prudently forbidden pilgrims to scratch or remove even the smallest piece of stone or mortar from the walls.

Another extraordinary event along the same lines occurred during the Council of Trent in 1562. Giovanni Suarez, Bishop of Coimbra, in Portugal, with the authorization of Pope Pius IV, had Father Francesco Stella extract a stone (still today encircled in iron on the right side of the altar), to place it in the foundations of a sanctuary modeled after the Loreto shrine, to be built in his diocese. On his way to Trent, the priest suffered a whole series of accidents and mishaps. The bishop, who enjoyed excellent health, was immediately struck by a strange illness that almost killed him. At that point, he received, through a nun, a supernatural message to have the stone returned to its place so he could get well again. He obeyed and sent Father Francesco Stella back to Loreto with the relic. The bishop was healed as soon as the stone was returned to its place. The prelate, repentant, wrote in his own hand a letter to the governor of Loreto, reporting the episode.[9]

---

8   Cit. in G. Gorel, *La santa Casa di Loreto*, cit., pp. 102-103.

9   Cf. O. Torsellini, *Lauretanae Historiae libri quinque*, Rome 1597, book IV, chap. 4. Torsellini "is considered the prince of the ancient Loreto historians" (Cf. G. Santarelli, *La Santa Casa di Loreto*, cit. p. 16.

Similar episodes occurred with other people, ec-
clesiastics, or simple believers, both for having stolen
stones and for having taken pieces of lime.[10]

In 1557, a German bishop fell ill for having accept-
ed as a gift a small stone removed by a soldier. He recovered only after returning the stolen good, still recog-
nizable today. In 1559, a gentleman returned a stone
that was stolen years earlier, after he lost his children,
property, and health because of the infraction. The same
happened to a Sicilian man in 1585. More recently, in
the twentieth century, after being hit by various changes
in circumstance and punishments, individual believers
had to give back what they had taken away, albeit out
of devotion.

Even Saint Therese of the Child Jesus confessed to
having had the temptation, during her 1887 pilgrimage,
to "furtively scratch the   walls sanctified by the divine
presence."[11]

1.2 Kisses on Walls, Kneeling
Around the House

All this indicates that the Holy House has always been the primary object of veneration and devotion in Loreto. It is no coincidence that, traditionally, the most common gesture is to kiss and touch
the sacred walls. Charles-Auguste de Sales recounts
that his uncle, Saint Francis de Sales, a pilgrim to
Loreto in 1599, once entered the Holy House, prostrated himself, and kissed the ground and the sacred
walls. Jacques Le Saige, a pilgrim in 1518, wrote: "I

10 Cf. G. Santarelli, *Tradizioni e leggende lauretane*, Edizioni Santa Casa, Loreto
2014, pp. 107-108.

11 Cit. in G. Santarelli, *Tradizioni e leggende lauretane*, cit., p. 109.

Photo: Longarini Bruno, Loreto.

Traditionally, before entering Mary's sacred cell, the pilgrims who came to Loreto walked the outer perimeter on their knees, reciting the rosary as they passed over the marble floor, which still shows two well-worn grooves dug by the knees of millions of pilgrims through the centuries.

believe that blessed Jesus, when he learned to walk, leaned against the wall of the said House. For our part, we touch our rosary beads to it."[12]

Moreover, when coming into contact with those stones one cannot but imagine the daily life of the Holy Family inside that dwelling. The stones actually seem just as worn as the lower part of the marble cover ordered by the popes to protect and exalt the Holy House. Traditionally, before entering the sacred cell of Mary, the pilgrims who came to Loreto walked along the outside perimeter on their knees, reciting the Rosary as they passed over the marble, which still clearly shows two furrows carved by the knees of millions of pilgrims over the centuries. This gesture had a penitential meaning, and was also meant to thank the Blessed Mother and ask favors. Unfortunately, for some decades, this is no longer customary, as many beautiful practices that forged the faith of Catholics for centuries are now seen as "outdated." On October 1, 1766, Pope Clement XIII granted an indulgence of seven years to anyone who went around the outside of the Holy House on his knees.

This devotion served to unite everyone, regardless of social class, age, or geographical origin. The chronicles tell us that, among others, the Queen of Poland, Maria Casimira, wife of John III Sobieski, the hero of Vienna against the Turks, while on pilgrimage to Loreto in 1698, humbly went around the outer part of the Holy House on her knees, along with other pilgrims.[13]

---

12 Cit. in *ibidem*, p. 104. More information on this topic has been taken from the same text.

13 Cf. G. Santarelli, *Tradizioni e leggende lauretane*, cit, pp. 97 & ff.

1.3 Why Is Our Lady's Statue Black?

Contrary to what one might think, the statue of Our Lady of Loreto, with its characteristic black color, has always played a secondary role, so to speak, concerning the Holy House itself. Reproductions of the Marian statue are certainly widespread across the world, but there are many other variants of the *Virgo Lauretana*, often associated with a house carried by angels. Therefore, the effigy of the Black Madonna is not the main theme when dealing with the Loreto issue. However, given the popularity it enjoys, especially in the Marche, let us dwell a bit on this point as well.

While in the past it was believed that the wooden statue had been present in the Holy House from the beginning with the features we still see today, a different study of the sources seems to indicate that at the time of the translation, an icon of Our Lady with Child was preserved between the sacred walls. The statue, made of spruce, dates back to the second half of the fourteenth century.

However, tradition has always attributed both representations to the evangelist St. Luke, known for his closeness to the Mother of God and referred to as the author of other images of the Virgin.

The black color of the statue is typical of the style and genre of black Madonnas. Many explain it by referring to the Song of Songs, of which these words are interpreted in a Marian key: "I am black but beautiful, O ye daughters of Jerusalem, as the tents of Cedar, as the curtains of Solomon. Do not consider me that I am brown, because the sun hath altered my color" (Cant 1:5-6). Or they refer to the *Turris eburnea* invocation of the Litany of Our Lady, which refers to the book of

"I am black but beautiful. O ye daughters of Jerusalem, as the tents of Cedar, as the curtains of Solomon. Do not consider that I am brown, because the sun has altered my color." (Cant 1:5-6)

Sirach, attributing this phrase to her: "I was exalted like a cedar in Lebanon" (Sir 24:17).

Another characteristic of the *Virgo Lauretana* is undoubtedly the dalmatic, a garment that goes from neck to feet and also covers arms and hands but does not directly touch the statue. Over time, the dress has had various reproductions and undergone several changes. However, the devotion of placing a black veil on the statue on Good Thursday and Friday (now only on Friday) has always been maintained. Afterward, the veil is cut up and given to pilgrims as a relic. Until 1797, when the *simulacrum*, with the ancient woolen robe that covered it, was raided by the French, a certificate was handed over to the faithful, attesting to the authenticity of that relic which touched the statue. It read: "I the undersigned Custodian of the Holy House of Loreto attest to the fact that the black veil sealed and attached to my signature, was worn by the Sacred Statue on Holy Thursday and Good Friday, and then touched to the Holy Dress and Holy Platter of the Blessed Virgin Mary, which is preserved in this Holy House. In faith, etc. Given in Loreto by the Custodian on this date..."[14]

In 1797, when Napoleon invaded and occupied Italy at the head of a revolutionary army, he stopped in Loreto and was responsible (as indeed in many other parts of the peninsula) for great looting of the shrine's treasure, so many riches and works of art have been irretrievably lost. Our Lady's statue was stolen and taken to the Louvre Museum in Paris. It remained there until 1802 when Pope Pius VII obtained its return. After keeping it for some time in the chapel of his Quirinale Palace, he had it solemnly transported to the Holy House on December 8 of that same year, a journey that

14 Cit. in G. Santarelli, *Tradizioni e leggende lauretane*, cit., p. 125.

crossed the provinces of Lazio and Umbria, finally arriving at the Marche.

On February 23, 1921, a fire in the cell of Our Lady of the Annunciation completely destroyed the wooden fourteenth-century statue, temporarily replaced with the same one used during the years of the French "captivity" of the original. Today it is kept in the convent of the nuns of the Visitation of Treia (Macerata).

On September 8, 1922, the new statue was placed in the Holy House. It is the same one we see today, blessed by Pope Pius XI, which he ordered carved in cedar wood from a tree in the Vatican gardens.[15] However, the black color of this statue is more uniform and accentuated than in the original.[16]

1.4 How Is the Holy House Furnished?

Noteworthy among the features of the Holy House is a small recessed opening located on the south wall beside the altar, where cruets are now stored. According to tradition,[17] it was the cupboard where Our Lady kept dishes and food. On the opposite side, in the same wall, is another recess with a small carved basin (no longer used), in which Mary washed her hands. On the right side of the altar, in front of the "cupboard," there is a wardrobe in which two cups are kept. In the imagination of the pilgrims, they were used by the Holy Family. But the piece that arouses the greatest devotion has always been the so-called bowl of baby Jesus, which scholars consider to date back to the time of Our

---

15 Cf. G. Santarelli, *Tradizioni e leggende lauretane*, cit., pp. 176 & ff.

16 Cf. *ibidem*, p. 168.

17 Cf. *ibidem*, pp. 112 & ff.

Lord's earthly life (first century AD).[18] Saint Therese of Lisieux wrote that she placed her rosary in it, a gesture of homage that the faithful performed. The bowl is now kept in the right corner of what is commonly called the "holy fireplace," located under the statue of Our Lady.

Finally, a wooden crucifix from the end of the thirteenth century hangs above the western wall window. Loreto historians such as Torsellini and Martorelli claim that it miraculously arrived with the three walls. They have written that since the crucifix is highly miraculous, the people of Recanati thought it was better to place it in a separate chapel in the sanctuary, which was done. However, the crucifix miraculously moved back to the Holy House. The faithful made a second attempt to relocate it, but failed; the crucifix "chose" to stay in Mary's abode. And there it stayed.[19]

1.5   Where Was the First Mass Celebrated?

Another important relic that arrived in Loreto with the Holy House is the so-called altar of the Apostles, now found on the east side under the marble altar where the Holy Mass is celebrated daily.

According to tradition, it is the altar the Apostles built in the sacred dwelling of Nazareth on which, according to Jacques Le Saige and Torsellini, Saint Peter celebrated the first Holy Mass.[20] It is truly evocative to offer the Holy Sacrifice and receive the Holy Eucharist right in the room where the Word became flesh. And it is just as edifying to imagine the Blessed Virgin Mary

---

18 Cf. G. Santarelli, *La Santa Casa di Loreto*, cit., p. 192.

19 Cf. G. Santarelli, *Tradizioni e leggende lauretane*, cit., p. 166.

20 Cf. N. Monelli-G. Santarelli, *L'altare degli Apostoli nella Santa Casa di Loreto*, Edizioni Santa Casa, Loreto 2012, pp. 23 & ff.

always receiving her Son really present with his Body, Blood, Soul and Divinity from the hands of the Apostles precisely in the same place where, decades earlier, she was greeted by the Angel and became the living tabernacle of Christ, and his monstrance for humanity.

Numerous witnesses attest to the existence of altars in Mary's home to celebrate Mass, certainly built over time, which they visited as pilgrims. Material tests confirm that the altar currently in Loreto dates back to the origins of the Church. The stones at its base and top have a herringbone pattern made with the Nabataean technique, the same style found in numerous stones of the Holy House.

From the sixteenth century, the altar was covered with marble, but following the terrible fire that broke out between February 23 and 24, 1921, Guido Cirilli, official architect of the sanctuary, had a new marble cover and altar made (the current one). The altar of the Apostles is now hardly visible, and only through a metal grid.

1.6 The House of Miracles

Should anyone think that the above is insufficient to attest to the authenticity of the Holy House, there are also the miracles that have occurred there over the ages and even to this day. Most are discrete, silent, and spiritual phenomena. But there have also been obvious and striking miracles. The amount of documentation on these irruptions of the supernatural in people's lives is so vast that it would fill entire volumes. Since it is impossible to list all the miracles here, let us have a general discussion, referring particularly to the most recent events, recalling specific works.[21]

---

21   Cf. for example, P. Cavatori, *Le guarigioni a Loreto. Gli sguardi e le carezze della Madonna*, Congregazione Universale della Santa Casa, Loreto 2001.

The so-called bowl of the Child Jesus, which scholars consider to date back to the time of Our Lord's earthly life (first century AD)

The so-called altar of the Apostles, now located on the east side under the marble altar where Holy Mass is celebrated daily.

A wooden crucifix from the end of the thirteenth century hangs above the window on the west wall.

From a chronological point of view, every century has recorded extraordinary facts about the Holy House. The sanctuary quickly became known throughout the world for the numerous healings that occurred there. Already in 1375, Pope Gregory XI recognized that, "because of the many miracles the Most High deigns to manifest therein, a great multitude of the faithful, moved by devotion, converge there."[22] Moreover, the votive offerings given to the sanctuary over the centuries are innumerable, a sign of the constant presence and attention of Our Lady for the children coming to her home. In addition to ordinary people, some of these miracles have involved famous personalities, sovereigns, popes, and saints. Later on, we will see, for example, the cases of Popes Pius II and Paul II, and of sovereigns like Louis XIII.

A noteworthy event is an exorcism that made it possible to find out exactly where the Holy Virgin and the Angel Gabriel were at the time of the Annunciation. In 1489, the noble Pierre Orgentorix, of Grenoble, tried by all means to free his wife Anna of the seven demons by which she was possessed. Despite exorcisms, nothing was achieved in France, and the family went to the Holy City of Rome, without results. Then they headed to the sanctuary of Loreto. The exorcisms practiced in the Holy House were so effective that even the demons admitted it, thanks to Our Lady, who showed herself particularly powerful in her former abode. Furthermore, the exorcist priest forced the last devil to leave the poor woman's body, and to point out Mary's and the Angel's exact positions at the time of the Incarnation. The devil declared that the Blessed Virgin was just beyond the altar, on the left side, while Gabriel stopped on the right

22   Cit. in *ibidem*, p. 5.

side of the window, keeping a distance out of respect for the immaculate purity of Our Lady.[23]

Among other miracles, we can recall the grace Our Lady of Loretto gave to St. Giacomo della Marca, who recovered from a blood leak and was able to continue his mission as a preacher. Or we recall the miracle worked for Christina, daughter of the king of Denmark and Duchess of Lorraine. She was taken on a stretcher to the Holy House, where she promptly regained her health. Other miracles happened with Jews and Muslims, who were converted to Catholicism. Another miracle recipient was the Frenchman Father Jean Jacques Olier, founder of the Society of Saint Sulpice. Suffering from a serious eye disease, he recovered after a pilgrimage on foot to the sanctuary.

Then there is the healing, in 1727, of Maria d'Angiò, who contributed to her Lutheran mother's conversion to Catholicism, and Calvinist Isacca Lamott, in 1732, who strangely lost her sight whenever she looked at the image of Our Lady in the Holy House. Once she promised to convert to the Catholic religion, her gaze was no longer prevented from seeing the statue of the Mother of God.

In the twentieth century, with the beginning of Unitalsi[24] pilgrimages to Loreto in white trains in 1936, many healings of sick Italians and foreigners took place. Just think of Mrs. Olga Spiridigliozzi,[25] healed in 2000 after a procession of the Blessed Sacrament in the square

---

23 Cf. P.V. Martorelli, *Teatro istorico della Santa Casa*, Roma 1732-1735, v. 1, pp. 346-347.

24 Italian National Union of Transport for the Ill to Lourdes and International Sanctuaries.

25 Cf. P. Cavatorti, *Le guarigioni a Loreto. Gli sguardi e le carezze della Madonna*, cit., pp. 138 & ff.

Countless are the ex-voto donated to the sanctuary over the centuries. In addition to ordinary people, some miracles involved notable personalities, kings, popes, and saints. Already in 1375, Pope Gregory XI recognized that "because of the many miracles the Most High deigns to manifest therein, a great multitude of the faithful, moved by devotion, converge there."

Pope Sixtus V had this inscription written on the facade of the basilica: "Deiparae domus in qua Verbum caro factum est" ("House of the Mother of God, in which the Word became flesh"), and "considering that numerous miracles are performed here for the countless believers who flock here from all over the world," he conferred on Loreto the title of city and bishopric.

outside the sanctuary. Innumerable extraordinary facts also occurred, not only after people passed between the holy walls, such as Elena Budellacci[26] in 1974, healed after twenty years of infirmity, but also from a distance, through prayer, seeing a statuette of Our Lady of Loreto, or using blessed oil from the sanctuary. For example, that was the case of Mr. Paul Holzgreve,[27] healed from a tetraparalysis between Christmas 1999 and January 2000 after an acquaintance brought him oil from the lamps of the Holy House and had it applied to his limbs.

---

26 Cf.   P. Cavatorti, *Le guarigioni a Loreto. Gli sguardi e le carezze della Madonna*, cit., pp. 133 & ff.

27 Cf. *ibidem*, pp. 125 & ff.

Chapter II

The House Brought by Angels

How did the Holy House arrive in Loreto?

In recent decades, some began to argue that the stones (mind you, the stones and not the walls, as has been always understood) of the Nazareth house were brought to Italy by men. Today, many have practically degraded the Angelic Translation of the Holy House on the Loreto hill to a pious legend. This operation is part of the process of continuous minimization of miraculous events, intended to make the Church "in sync" with the times, to become more credible in the eyes of the world. In reality, however, this attitude undermines people's faith.

As we will see in a moment, the "modern" version of the Loreto question is more than doubtful. Notwithstanding the fact that it is not a dogma of faith, Pope Saint John Paul II sent an Apostolic Letter to celebrate the 7th Centenary of Loreto, in which he expressed the desire to allow "historical research full freedom to investigate the origin of the Sanctuary and Loreto tradition." It is precisely this freedom that entitles us to continue to think that the traditional version of the miraculous translation is scientifically based and much more reasonable.

Father Giuseppe Santarelli is a historian of the Loreto question from whose works we have drawn extensively because of the amount of valuable information they provide. He presents this new human transport thesis only as a hypothesis, without any incontrovertible certainty, though tending to support it. Other scholars, such as Prof. Giorgio Nicolini, have also raised this hypothesis.

In the preface to Santarelli's work, Bishop Giovanni Tonucci, papal delegate to Loreto from 2007 to 2017, while reiterating freedom of historical research, writes that "persons who look down on those who love the beautiful tradition of angelic transport almost as if it were a superficial credulity are in error."[28]

Now let us try to understand why the miraculous translation is neither a pious invention nor a superficial credulity.

2.1 Historically Ascertained Translations

Historically, at least five miraculous translations of the Holy House of Nazareth have been ascertained. They took place over a period ranging from 1291 to 1296 in Trsat (now a district of the city of Fiume), Ancona (Posatora), in the forest of Lady Loreta (now known as Banderuola), on a field of two brothers located on Mount Prodo (in front of the current sanctuary of Loreto) and on a public road on which the basilica now stands and where a city was built around the distinguished relic.[29]

---

28   G. Santarelli, *La Santa Casa di Loreto*, cit., pp. 6-7.

29   Cf. G. Nicolini, "Le cinque traslazioni 'miracolose' della Santa Casa di Nazareth," in *Il segno del soprannaturale*, no. 216, June 2006, p. 28.

While that does not mean the holy walls of Nazareth could not have been to other places, there are no historical-archaeological documents in this regard. However, local folk traditions of Tuscany, Umbria, and Marche suggest that in the period starting with Trsat (December 9-10, 1294) and before arriving in Ancona (1295), the Holy House traveled and perhaps stayed in various locations in central Italy.[30] It is no coincidence that people in the Marches speak of her "coming," in Umbria, of her "passage," and in some areas of Tuscany, of her "great journey." These different ways of naming the same miraculous event were handed down from generation to generation. Moreover, it is precisely in these areas that the Ancient Via Lauretana and the so-called Loreto roads are located. Therefore, it is possible that the Holy House made short stops.

There are very valid reasons for believing that the five above-mentioned moves are authentic.

But why would the Holy House have left Palestine?

The three walls disappeared from the Basilica of the Annunciation in Nazareth in the same year (1291) in which the Crusaders, defeated in St. John of Acre, had to definitively abandon the Holy Land. Indeed, it has always been said that the miraculous translation took place to preserve the Holy House from Islamic rule. It would, therefore, be a clear signal that the Holy House was defended against the conquest of the Muslim world. As we will see later, this theme is very linked to Loreto.

It is very significant that this great relic of Christendom from the Holy Land chose the territory of the Papal States, governed by the Vicar of Christ, as its ultimate destination.

---

30 Cf. G. Santarelli, *Tradizioni e Leggende Lauretane*, cit., p. 161.

William Garratt, a professor of art at the University of Cambridge, a convert from Anglicanism, and great historian of Loreto,[31] asked himself a question a knight would ask in the Holy Land, wondering if God would ever allow Muslims to turn the Holy House into a mosque. "No, the Lord will not suffer this," he replied. "If need be, the Holy House will no longer be found there. God will know how to withdraw it from profanation or destruction. ... The Christian power in Palestine may be entirely overthrown; not a single soldier of the

31 Author of *Loreto, The New Nazareth and Its Centenary Jubilee* (1893).

Representation of the successive translations of the Holy House. Anonymous author, sixteenth century. Pinacoteca Museum, Loreto.

Cross may remain to defend the sacred walls wherein God became man; the fanaticism of the followers of the false prophet may profane all other Christian churches; but the Omnipotent can limit the blind fury of unbelievers; and when there are no human hands and hearts to protect the hallowed Chamber of the Incarnation, God will give His Angels charge over it; if necessary, in their hands they shall bear it up; they shall snatch it away from profanation, and it shall be found in a Christian land, where it shall be venerated." [32]

32 Cit. in G. Gorel, *La santa Casa di Loreto*, cit., pp. 49-50. Cf. also
    https://archive.org/stream/LoretoTheNewNazareth/LoretoTheNewNazareth_
    djvu.txt

2.2   The Triple Miracle in the First Translation

It is impossible not to point out the triple miracle that took place on the night of the first translation, May 9-10, 1291, when the Holy House disappeared from the Basilica of the Annunciation in the Holy Land. The precious relic was located underneath the building, in the crypt, and had already been preserved from the Islamic destruction in 1263, perpetrated by Alan ed-Din Taybar, Lieutenant of the Sultan of Cairo Bajbars Banokan. In 1291, however, how could the three walls get off their foundations and leave the church basement, and so quickly?

Suddenly, in the space of one night, the holy walls were uprooted and disappeared from the basement of the Basilica, where they had been protected, and arrived in Istria. The Holy House had been in its original place until May 9, 1291; the next day, May 10, it was no longer there, without anyone being able to give any explanation. What happened? Had it been a human operation, how was it possible to do that job in such a short time, that is, to take the walls off their foundations, get them out of the protective crypt without taking them apart, and transport them in a single night thousands of miles away, to Trsat? Had this been a "human translation," on whose orders or permission was it carried out, since there were no documents or testimonies in this regard?

2.3   Two Ancient Plaques

We must also bear in mind the testimony of Blessed Giovanni Battista Spagnoli, known as the Mantuan. On a visit to the sanctuary of Loreto, this famous and influential Carmelite religious read a very ancient plaque attached to church walls, telling the story of the translations. As in earlier testimonies by Pier Giorgio Tolomei, known as Il Teramano, Governor of the Holy House (in 1472) and Giacomo Ricci (in 1469), in a letter of September 22, 1489 to Cardinal Girolamo Della Rovere (or in 1479, according to some) written in the Mantuan dialect, he said, "Having recently come to the Holy House of the Blessed Virgin Mary of Loreto and seen the admirable things that God works in that place ... I began to observe everything with diligence, to admire and read the huge number of *ex voto* (a religious offering given in order to express devotion or gratitude) posted on the walls. And behold my eyes fall on an old plaque corroded by age and long exposure, in which is written the reason why that place has reached such great fame. Led by a pious zeal to prevent the carelessness of men (which usually obscures even the most distinguished things) from losing the memory of such a marvelous episode, I copied from that plaque, consumed by woodworm and dust, the series of events," or miraculous translations of the Holy House of Nazareth to various places, and finally, to Loreto.[33]

Spagnoli continues: "All the things we have said above, with the exception of very few which clarify but do not alter history, have been taken from an authentic copy of the aforementioned plaque, to which faith must be borne, always supposing that the writing is true."[34] Therefore, at the time of writing (second half of the fifteenth century), there were two plaques: one corroded by time, and a more readable copy. This means that the history of the miraculous translations is not a tale created at that time. The two plaques, which necessarily received ecclesiastical approval to stay in the church,

---

33 Cit. in G. Nicolini, *La veridicità storica della miracolosa traslazione della Santa Casa di Nazareth a Loreto*, La Voce Cattolica, Ancona 2004, pp. 25-26.

34 Cit. in *ibidem*, p. 26.

were certainly very old. According to some scholars,[35] the oldest plaque was the work of Blessed Pietro Moluzzi, bishop of Macerata, to whose diocese Pope John XXII aggregated the territory of Recanati and therefore Loreto in 1320, entrusting him with the custody of the Holy House. Furthermore, according to reports from ancient texts and authors, the same Blessed Pietro Moluzzi, a living witness to the miraculous translations, was the author of a first written history which was used in school lessons to instruct the faithful and the new generations about the extraordinary events that happened in that blessed place. Although the original manuscript no longer exists, extracts from the text of Blessed Pietro Moluzzi or copies of it are found in many ancient books, written by authors who had the opportunity to consult and quote the originals.

In the Archives of the Canons of Loreto one finds the *Cronichetta della Santa Casa* (Little Chronicle of the Holy House), printed in 1844, which confirms the antiquity of written testimony dating back to the origins of the miraculous events. It mentions a document from 1324 belonging to the State Archive of Padua, which reads: "*Triginta abhinc annis Domus Beatae Virginis Mariae de Nazareth per manus Angelorum translata fuit per mare Adriaticum prope Urbem Recineti*" – "Thirty years ago, the House of the Blessed Virgin Mary of Nazareth was transported by the Angels through the Adriatic Sea near the city of Recanati." The *Little Chronicle of the Holy House,* which quotes from that document, was authored by Canon Raffaele Sinibaldi, chaplain of the Royal House of Bourbon. He asserts that the authentic text of that very important document was presented to H.E. Most Rev. Stefano Bellini,

---

35 Cf. *ibidem*, p. 27.

Bishop of Loreto, while the latter was writing a history of the Holy House.

2.4 First Leg: Trsat

Trsat, now a district of the city of Rijeka, in Croatia, was the first place where the Holy House came to rest after leaving Nazareth. A sanctuary dedicated to Our Lady is still standing there, built in memory of the holy abode's stay. The miraculous event dates back to the night between May 9 and 10, 1291.

The link between Trsat and Loreto over the centuries has always been very strong. It is no coincidence that the Illyrian Palace (Illyricum is the ancient name of Croatia), dedicated to the formation of Croatian and Albanian clerics, was built in the sixteenth century in the square of the Marche sanctuary. Furthermore, pilgrims from across the Adriatic have always been numerous in Loreto.

At Trsat, testimonies of the coming of the Holy House are innumerable. Halfway along the monumental staircase that leads to the sanctuary, in front of one of the chapels lining the steps, one finds these words carved on marble, probably dating back to the 14th century: "The House of the Blessed Virgin Mary came from Nazareth to Trsat in the year 1291, on the 10th of May, and departed on the 10th of December, 1294."[36]

According to a report by the Istrian Franciscan Francesco Glavinich, in his *Historia Tersattana*,[37] some woodcutters saw on the morning of May 10, 1291, a building in a clearing of the forest then present on that territory they had never seen before. It was a small house, with an altar inside. The event did not go unnoticed, and

---

36   Cit. in G. Gorel, *La santa Casa di Loreto*, cit., p. 51.

37   For a summary, cf. G.M. Pace, *Miracolosa traslazione a Loreto della dimora della Santissima Annunziata*, cit., pp. 8 & ff.

news of the discovery promptly spread and reached the local parish priest, Fr. Alessandro Giorgiewich, who was bedridden and seriously ill with dropsy. Eager to see with his own eyes the small building that mysteriously arrived in the territory of his parish, the priest prayed to Our Lady, who appeared to him, healed him, and informed him that the walls in question were those of her Nazareth residence, which had been preserved from profanation by the infidels.

"Know," said Mary Most Holy, "that I was born in this house; here I grew up in my early childhood. Here, at the annunciation of the archangel Gabriel, I conceived the Divine Son through the work of the Holy Spirit. Here the Word became flesh. The apostles consecrated this dwelling and celebrated the august sacrifice in it ... God, to whom nothing is impossible, is the author of this miracle and so that you may become its witness and apostle, be healed. Your sudden return to health after such a long disease will confirm this miracle." [38]

Given the exceptional nature of the event, the viceroy of the area, Nicola Frangipani, sent a four-man delegation to Nazareth, including Fr. Giorgiewich himself, to make sure that it really was the Holy House of Our Lady. The envoys were able to ascertain that the walls of the dwelling where the Incarnation took place were no longer in the Basilica of the Annunciation. Only their foundations remained, the perimeter of which matched exactly that of the walls gone to Trsat. Everything was put in writing, with a notarial deed, and preserved.

However, between December 9 and 10, 1294, the three walls left Croatia just as mysteriously as they had arrived three and a half years before. Then, a small chapel was built as a reminder that Our Lady's house had stayed there. In 1420, Pope Martin V granted indulgences to all

---

38   Cit. in G. Gorel, *La santa Casa di Loreto*, cit., p. 53.

Representation of the successive translations of the Holy House. Anonymous author, sixteenth century. Pinacoteca Museum, Loreto. The author of this work paints cities idealized in a medieval manner, and the armies of the Duke of Urbino wearing the military uniform of the sixteenth century. Our Lady's House appears in Nazareth surrounded by walls (1), attacked by infidels. In a second representation (2), it is transported by angels, and in a third, (3) the House, now in safety, rests in another walled city across the sea. (Museum of the Vice Kingdom of Mexico)

Trsat in Croatia, today a district of Rijeka, was the first place where the Holy House rested after leaving Nazareth. A sanctuary dedicated to Our Lady in memory of the Holy House's sojourn still stands there.

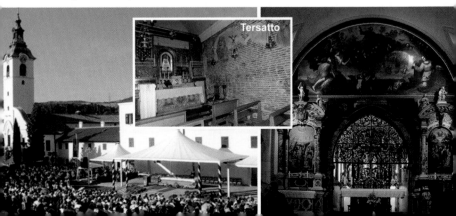

Tersatto

those who contributed to the maintenance of the Croatian sanctuary. Pope Nicholas V, when accepting the Franciscans as custodians of the church, called it a place of worship made famous in past centuries. Pope Urban V, who arrived in Loreto in 1367, was able to see the pain of many Croatian pilgrims who still mourned the departure of the Holy House from their land ("Come, come back to us with your house, beautiful Lady," was the most common lament).[39] To console them for that serious loss, the Pontiff gave them a statue of Our Lady to be placed in their sanctuary in Trsat.[40]

However, the sadness of Croatians has persisted over the centuries as a supreme attestation of the authenticity of that residence of the Most Holy Virgin. Citing Father Riera, Martorelli recounts a massive pilgrimage in 1559, when five hundred men and women from Trsat went around the church and Holy House on their knees, as customary, holding lit candles in their hands and repeating aloud, all together: "Come, come back to us, O Mary, come back because you are abandoning us."[41]

Moreover, in addition to Trsat, devotion to Our Lady of Loreto remains very much alive throughout Croatia.[42]

2.5 Second Leg: Ancona

According to tradition, after its departure from Trsat, the Holy House arrived in Ancona, which at the time was the most important seaport of the Papal States.

---

39 Cf. P.V. Martorelli, *Teatro istorico della Santa Casa*, cit., v. 2, capo 4, p. 353.

40 Cf. G.M. Pace, *Miracolosa traslazione a Loreto della dimora della Santissima Annunziata*, cit., p. 29.

41 P.V. Martorelli, *Teatro istorico della Santa Casa*, cit., v. 2, capo 4, p. 353.

42 Just to give one example, in May 2017 on the hill named Gaj of Primôsten, a 55-foot-tall statue of Our Lady of Loreto (including the access stairs and pedestal) was inaugurated (Cf. *Il Messaggio della Santa Casa*, n. 7, luglio-agosto 2017, p. 269).

In 1295, it stayed for nine months in the capital of the Marche region, as attested to by Father Matteo, a priest who was contemporary to the events. He left a document of which only a copy remained, found in 1732 in the box of "authentic relics" that still exists in the Cathedral of Ancona. In the years following the miraculous translations, Father Matteo left a text for personal devotion, so the memory of that prodigious event in Ancona would not be lost. The city inhabitants also built a little chapel on a hill overlooking the port, where the Holy House had stayed.

The handwritten document reads: "I, Father Matteo, pastor of St. Onoufrius outside the Campo di Marte Gate of the city of Ancona, out of devotion leave this memory of this miracle, which occurred in the year 1295. The Holy House of the Mother of God settled in the forest around the Posatore neighborhood for nine months; and since I was very dismayed that so few people had remained because of great wars and plagues, I decided to put this written reminder under the sacred stone of the Church of Saint Catherine. May the Blessed Virgin grant that it will be found in the appropriate time. A most humble servant of God."[43]

Even stronger evidence of the miraculous event is the construction by local bishops of three churches in memory of the Holy House's sojourn on Ancona's Posatora hill and its subsequent translations to the Recanati area.

One of the three churches, in the town of Barcaglione (on the hills between Ancona and Falconara Marittima), still stands in the same place where local inhabitants saw the Holy House flying in from the sea.

---

43   Cit. in G. Nicolini, *La veridicità storica della miracolosa traslazione della Santa Casa di Nazareth a Loreto* cit., p. 53. Note that, as Nicolini himself observed (p. 54), the church of St. Onoufrios was very close to that of St. Catherine, and the area of Posatora was part of the same parish jurisdiction.

For its part, the current church of Posatora stands on the same hilly area where the Holy House stayed for nine months. The place's telltale name derives from the Latin, *"posat et ora"* ("land and pray"), meaning that Our Lady's dwelling landed there, where she prayed for the city, and was prayed to by the population.

Finally, even more important is the construction next to the Cathedral of San Ciriaco of the church of Santa Maria of Nazareth in the early 1300s, which has disappeared due to the destruction of war. It was consecrated by the Bishop of Ancona, a contemporary witness of the translations, to recall and liturgically celebrate all the miraculous translations of the Holy House.

Furthermore, two marble plaques were set in the church of Posatora attesting to the miracle that took place there. One is from the thirteenth and fourteenth centuries and existed until the mid-twentieth century. Unfortunately, it was lost due to restoration work, but there are living eyewitnesses who remember and bear witness to its existence. The other plaque, evidently translated and copied from the first one, dates back to 1545 and is still present in the church. It reads: "In this forest, the Holy House of the Mother of God rested for nine months. MCCXCV." The first plaque, in the legible part which the witnesses remember, recited in ancient popular Latin, *"Quita futa reposata la Madonna di Loreta* ("this is where Loreta's Blessed Virgin came after landing").[44] Interestingly, the term "Loreta" already indicates the place in the forest of Signora Loreta of the subsequent miraculous translation.

---

44 Cf. G. Nicolini, *La veridicità storica della miracolosa traslazione della Santa Casa di Nazareth a Loreto* cit., pp. 57-58. Cf. anche G. Nicolini, *Le cinque traslazioni "miracolose" della Santa Casa di Nazareth*, cit., pp. 28 & ff.

The church of Santa Maria Liberatrice was built in the sixteenth century on a previous sacred building of the thirteenth century. According to the existing historical and archaeological documents, during their journey accompanying the Holy House from Nazareth to the Marche, the angels "laid" the three walls of the Holy House of Nazareth for nine months exactly where this church stands today.

2.6 Third Leg: the Forest of Signora Loreta

Still in 1295, the three walls of the Holy House arrived at a grove in the Recanati area located behind the current Loreto railway station.[45] That wild and marshy place was the property of a noble lady of Recanati called Loreta, from which derives the name of the town that houses the sanctuary. Today, a small church stands as a memorial in the area where the precious relic landed. The place is called "Banderuola" because at the time of the miraculous events, some devotees hoisted a flag on the top of a very high pine to show pilgrims from faraway the exact point where the Holy House was located.

Our Lady's dwelling stayed in this place for a few months, as attested by the said ancient plaque exposed in the Holy House, which was mentioned in the studies of

---

45 Cf. G. Nicolini, *La veridicità storica della miracolosa traslazione della Santa Casa di Nazareth a Loreto* cit., p. 68.

Teramano (1472) and Blessed Giovanni Battista Spagno-li (1479). Moreover, Teramano received under oath the testimony of two elderly inhabitants of the place, Paolo di Rinalduzio and Francesco il Priore.[46] The former reported he knew that an ancestor of his had seen with his own eyes the Holy House coming in flight from the sea and landing in the forest. The latter declared that one of his ancestors had visited the Holy House when it was still on the property of Signora Loreta and witnessed its miraculous translation to Mount Prodo. One could certainly smile at these testimonies, deeming them superficial and unconvincing. However, given the seriousness of the writer reporting them, there are no valid reasons to disregard them.

In addition to the two Teramano witnesses, the miraculous event was confirmed by Saint Nicholas of Tolentine, who attested to the arrival of the Holy House, and Friar Paolo della Selva, a hermit who lived on the nearby Montorso hill and had a supernatural revelation on the true origin of the three walls.[47]

The pilgrims immediately began to flow into that sacred place despite the absence of any utilities or hospitality. Their faith and enthusiasm were so great that they would rather pray and camp day and night under trees than leave. The Mantuan wrote that pilgrims also came from faraway regions. However, all this influx caused problems. As Ricci explains in his *Historia Virginis Mariae Loretae* (fifteenth century), brigands and criminals flocked to the area to rob devotees, making it impossible to visit the Holy House. That was obviously the main reason for its new move, this time a little higher up, on Mount Prodo.

---

46   Cf. G. Nicolini, *Le cinque traslazioni "miracolose" della Santa Casa di Nazareth*, Il segno del soprannaturale, no. 220, October 2006, pp. 28-29.

47   Cf. G. Gorel, *La santa Casa di Loreto*, cit., pp. 62 & ff.

However, miracles continued to occur in that place. Witnesses and historians like Riera and Angelita recount that the area in which the Holy House had settled for eight months continued to have flowers and grass, unlike its surroundings, invaded by bushes and thorns. Unfortunately, those miraculous signs were erased when local farmers inadvertently began clearing the area and working the land. In 1575, when Pope Gregory XIII ordered the reclamation of the area, the trees, which for three hundred years had bent towards the sea, where the House of the Blessed Mother had come, were felled. However, as mentioned, a chapel was built on the site, which stands to this day.

Regarding the "miracle of the trees," we believe it useful for the reader to consider the 1790 report by Father Antonio Gudenti, a patrician of Osimo and archdeacon of the Loreto Basilica. He literally cites the famous Torsellini, a witness closer to the events. In chapter six of the first book of his monumental work, *Lauretanae Historiae libri quinque*, he writes: "Famously (and it is no vain belief), at the arrival of the House of Mary, a long line of trees bowed upon its passage and remained that way as witnesses to the miracle until they fell due to old age, the force of wind, or were cut down. The memory of it is still fresh, the same author continues, and I can assure you that a very trustworthy man ascertained to me that, at the age of twenty, he often saw many of these with their trunks bent towards the sea. When the woods around them were cut down, they were left standing there out of respect for the event. However, at a later date, out of foolishness or inexperience, peasants cut them down so they would not hinder the plow."[48]

---

48   Cit. in A. Gaudenti, *Storia della Santa Casa di Loreto esposta in dieci brevi ragionamenti fra un sacerdote custode di S. Casa ed un divoto pellegrino*, ed. seconda, Loreto 1790, p. 41.

2.7   Fourth Leg:the Field of Two Brothers

The three walls then reached Mount Prodo, where at the time there was nothing but a few trees and a small house. This time, the chosen place was a field belonging to a couple of brothers, Simon and Stefano Rinaldi of the Ancients.[49] While it is difficult to identify the exact point where the Holy House landed, it is known to have been in front of what is today the sanctuary. In fact, a small carved stone is still on the wall at the end of the current Apostolic Palace, which depicts an image of Our Lady sitting on the Holy House. Below is the inscription "*visitatio custodivit*" ("this place watched the visit" of the Holy House).

However, the two brothers, albeit very happy to have been so privileged by Divine Providence, soon began to quarrel. The numerous pilgrims flocking to the sacred dwelling left rich votive gifts to honor the Mother of God. The two, taken by greed, entered into conflict. The situation became so problematic that the Municipality of Recanati turned to Pope Boniface VIII, who was informed and aware of the miraculous translations, as attested in the eighteenth century by the aforementioned Bishop of Montefeltro, Valerio Martorelli. The pope was asked to resolve the dispute and perhaps expropriate the land from the brothers and make it public soil. In reality, no intervention was needed because, in December of 1296, the Holy House left that field and landed where it is now venerated. That was its fifth and last translation.

---

49 Cf.   G. Nicolini, *Le cinque traslazioni 'miracolose' della Santa Casa di Nazareth*, Il segno del soprannaturale, no. 222, December 2006, pp. 28-29.

Brigands and criminals began to attack, robbing devotees and making it impossible to visit the Holy House. This was obviously the main reason for the new move, this time a little higher, on Mount Prodo. Marble cladding by Antonio da Sangallo, 1531-1534

2.8 Fifth Leg: the Public Road

At the end of 1296, "through the angelic minis-try," the Holy House came to rest in the middle of a public road that connected Recanati with Ancona and Porto Recanati. The three walls placed themselves in the street, without any foundation. A large wall was built around it only when the lack of foundations was deemed unsafe. The most basic common sense would suffice to understand that the placement of the Holy

In 1295, the Holy House's three walls landed on a grove in the Recanati area, located behind the current Loreto railway station. Today a small church stands on the place as a reminder. The place is called "weather vane" because some devotees, at the time of the miraculous events, hoisted a flag on the top of a very tall pine tree to show pilgrims the exact spot where the Holy House was.

QUI
OVE AL TRAMONTO DEL XIII SECOLO
RICHIAMATE DA CANDIDA "BANDERUOLA„
ONDEGGIANTE SULLA VETTA D'ALTISSIMO PINO
CONVENIVANO DIVOTE LE GENTI
A VENERARE L'UMILE CASA DEL VERBO INCARNATO
PORTATA IN VOLO DAGLI ANGELI
LE NUOVE GENERAZIONI
RICORDANDO IL GRANDE PRODIGIO
GLORIA E VANTO DELLA TERRA PICENA
CON LA FEDE DEI PADRI
IMPLORANO DA DIO GRAZIE E BENEDIZIONI
ALLE FAMIGLIE ALLA PATRIA

+ G.M. MCMXLIV

House on the public road was not the work of humans. Indeed, how to explain that the local authorities could have allowed a building to be erected in an important public road at the cost of remaking a considerable section of it? What is more, why was the building erected without any foundations, a supposed omission later remedied with successive works much more demanding and expensive than would have been the common foundation of any other building?

2.9 Some Clarifications

As far as dates are concerned, 1294 is generally and conventionally considered the year in which the Holy House arrived in Loreto. However, the only certainty is that the precious relic left Trsat and arrived on Italian soil in that year. According to Prof. Giorgio Nicolini,[50] the error is due to Recanati's archivist, Girolamo Angelita, who in the sixteenth century, set the date of arrival in Loreto as December 10, 1294, confusing the date of the Holy House's disappearance from Trsat (precisely December 10, 1294) with that of its arrival in the Recanati area, where Loreto then arose.

Now, concerning the attestation of the authenticity of the miraculous translations that took place in those years, it is well to note the construction of the church of Forio, on the island of Ischia. In 1295, after local fishermen returning from Ancona brought the news about the Holy House, the inhabitants of Forio began to build a church dedicated to miracles that occurred in the Marche region. They built the church even before these miraculous events had their conclusion (in 1296),

---

50 Cf. G. Nicolini, *La veridicità storica della miracolosa traslazione della Santa Casa di Nazareth a Loreto* cit., pp. 78-79.

a sign that there was a widespread knowledge of the great event already at the time.[51]

2.10 Angels? Or the Angeli Family?

At this point, it is necessary to make some clarifications about the modern version of the story of the Holy House of Loreto that seems to have almost completely supplanted the traditional one, officially recognized by the authority of the Church and by the faithful for centuries. This version claims that the Holy House's miraculous angelic flight was simply an elaborate popular reworking of a merely human event - albeit assisted by Divine Providence - attributable instead to a certain family by the name of Angeli or De Angelis.

Those who support this hypothesis (because it is a mere hypothesis) refer to the presumed historical source, the so-called *Chartularium Culisanense*. This is a collection of documents of various types of which the originals have disappeared, and only a copy (true or presumed to be true) from 1859 remains at the Marcogliano Library Institution of the monks of Montevergine (Avellino).

According to a publication by Prof. Andrea Nicolotti, which we will discuss shortly, this document is an historical forgery created in the nineteenth century by a family with the surname De Angelis from Culisano (Palermo), to make believe that its lineage derived from the "Angeli," a princely family of Epirus.

Page 181 of this false document lists the dowry property, brought by Ithamar, daughter of the despot of Epirus Nicephorus I Angeli-Comnenus, to Philip of Anjou, Prince of Taranto and son of the King of Naples,

---

51 Cf. *ibidem*, pp. 80-81.

Charles II of Anjou, on the occasion of their marriage in 1294. Among these assets, we note "holy stones" taken from the house of Our Lady ("*sanctas petras ex domo Dominae Nostrae Deiparae ablatas*"), along with a wooden table painted with her image, holding the Infant Jesus.

Even if one were to admit (just for the sake of argument) the authenticity of that document, its claim that some stones were taken "from the Holy House" does not at all mean that it is referring to the House of Nazareth, as the Virgin lived in several houses during her life (in Jerusalem, Egypt, Ephesus). In any case, the document speaks only of "holy stones taken away" and therefore does not refer to the Holy House as a whole but only some stones! Instead, in Loreto, one finds the Holy House "intact," and not merely "some stones" of it. Furthermore, it has always been known and understood that the intact walls of Mary's room miraculously left Nazareth, rather than individual stones. If this were about mere stones, it would be absurd to speak of the "Holy House," since in Loreto today one would not see part of Our Lady's house, but simply some stones taken from it.

Furthermore, many questions remain unexplained. Why was Nicephorus I Angeli-Comnenus able to dispose of the famous relic, then located under the Basilica of the Annunciation? No local ecclesiastical authority had anything to say? Even admitting that transport operations were designed to preserve the house from Islamic violence (the conquest of St. John of Acre took place in 1291), why did these assets then end up in the territory of Loreto, which at the time was part of the State of the Church? Why is nothing known about this journey, which would certainly have required money, time, and organization? [52]   The most widespread hypothesis, which lacks a solid foundation, speaks of a gift to the pontiff. However, although stones in different quantities and weights could be transported by sea (but not an entire house), it is impossible to explain why the relic moved five times and was reconstructed with all its truly exceptional characteristics (without foundations, with Middle Eastern mortar, and dating back to many centuries ago, set on a public road and lying partly on-air, etc.).

It is not surprising that the translation or, better, the "miraculous transfers" of the Holy House have been questioned by people with materialist, rationalist, and skeptical minds regarding any supernatural intervention. This mentality has been present since the advent of humanism during the Renaissance period.

For his part, Prof. Nicolini denounces some present-day scholars who misleadingly interpret paintings, depictions, and xylographs of the fifteenth and sixteenth centuries, suggesting that they already show the two "hypotheses" -- human transport and miraculous transport.

One such example is a sixteenth century painting preserved in the Museum-Picture Gallery of the Shrine. Since it is a sort of geographical map, this painting depicts seafaring ships and the Holy House carried by angels over the sea. The author's intention is well illustrated in the caption below, which expressly states that the painting is only about the "miraculous translations," and the ships are only an embellishment of the work. Moreover, that which some today identify as the

---

52   Cf. G.M. Pace, *Miracolosa traslazione a Loreto della dimora della Santissima Annunziata*, cit., pp. 18 & ff.

"Holy House" is actually the shed that medieval ships had on their bow to keep the tools used for navigation. However, books by some recent scholars publish only the sheds without the unequivocal description of the author, leading readers to believe that the painting seeks to represent the two "hypotheses": miraculous transport and human transport, naturally giving more credit to the latter hypothesis than the former.

The same happens with a print from 1582-1585, preserved in the Uffizi in Florence: the tiny detail of a ship with a house and without a sail proves nothing, if only because the author, also in this case, writes below some notes speaking exclusively of the miraculous transport.

Therefore, the existence of skeptics on the Loreto question, as on many other events, cannot invalidate its historical veracity. Moreover, if in the past the deniers focused more on the authenticity of the Holy House, it was roughly at the beginning of the twentieth century, with Canon Ulisse Chevalier, that people began to talk about maritime transport and therefore human transport of the House. But the ecclesiastical authority has always distanced itself from this hypothesis, which several Catholic authors have denied in many texts, as we will see shortly.

Back to the *Chartularium Culisanense*, in a 2012 study, Prof. Andrea Nicolotti,[53] of the Department of Historical Studies of the University of Turin, greatly downplayed the allegedly decisive importance of the document, the authenticity of which he doubts. In his conclusions, while stating he is unable to take a clear

---

53 Cf. A. Nicolotti, *Su alcune testimonianze del Chartularium Culisanense, sulle false origini dell'Ordine Costantiniano Angelico di Santa Sofia e su taluni suoi documenti conservati presso l'Archivio di Stato di Napoli*, in www.lavocecattolica.it/falseorigini.cartularium.pdf 2012.

position on the subject for lack of evidence, he clearly states that in his opinion, "the substantially false character of the Byzantine history and documents produced by the De Angelis family [of Palermo, in whose palace the *Chartularium* was found, and who have no connection with the rulers of Epirus] must render the credibility of all the sources they accredit strongly suspect."[54] If this is true, the whole hypothesis of human transport and popular reworking of the Angeli Family into heavenly angels is blatantly false.

The discovery of two coins in the basement of the Holy House, minted by the Angeli family and datable between 1287 and 1308, is not sufficient to support that hypothesis.[55] First, because in it were found hundreds of coins of various ages and even from Roman times (in ancient times, there was a necropolis in that place), as people normally left donations during their pilgrimage. Second, the presence of coins attests, if anything, to a gesture of devotion by some pilgrims but certainly not that the building was transported by humans and reconstructed in that place. On the contrary, the presence of those coins and five red fabric crosses that belonged to the crusaders, only confirms the authenticity of the Holy House, which arrived in the Marche region at the end of the thirteenth century.

Equally inconsistent are allusions to alleged documents in the Vatican Secret Archives[56] dating between the late nineteenth and early twentieth centuries that were hidden or destroyed. They are said to have denied the thesis of the miraculous transportation of the House

---

54   A. Nicolotti, cit., p. 17.

55   Cf. G. Nicolini, *La veridicità storica della miracolosa traslazione della Santa Casa di Nazareth a Loreto* cit., pp. 47-48.

56   Cf. G. Nicolini, *La veridicità storica della miracolosa traslazione della Santa Casa di Nazareth a Loreto* cit., pp. 44-45.

of Mary, theretofore supported by the Church and all popes. This rumor was spread at the time of Pope Leo XIII by the then-bishop of Dijon, Most Rev. Maurice Landrieux, who supposedly learned about it from the papal physician, Giuseppe Lapponi,[57] a skeptic on everything concerning Loreto. However, there is no proof to corroborate this claim, which is nothing but hearsay, likely spread by people interested in sowing confusion. How is it possible that no enemy of the Loreto question, including Lapponi, ever managed to prove anything over so many years?

In short, although everything remains enveloped in a certain mystery, the same can be said of countless other events in sacred history and recent miracles, speaking today of a "miraculous translation" of the Holy House still appears as the most rational and reasonable solution, and we do not see why certain Catholic circles should display such fury against it.

2.11 The Mysterious Night between December 9 and 10

Further attestation of the miraculous translation is found in folk festivals. Our Lady of Loreto is the patron saint of the Marches, and December 10, the day in which the translation of the Holy House is remembered liturgically, was also proclaimed by the civil institutions "Marche Day."

Unfortunately, following the profound social and cultural changes that have taken place since the end of the 1960s, many secular traditions linked to this feast have been lost. However, in recent times, we have witnessed their recovery, dictated especially by a desire to

57   Cf. G. Santarelli, *La Santa Casa di Loreto*, cit., pp. 211 & ff.

Many churches in the Marche region preserve typical sculptural sets, usually in wood, depicting the Holy House shaped as church and equipped with a small bell tower with the Virgin and Child above.

Collegiate Church of St. Secondo, Asti

"Fires of the Coming" and procession in Loreto

preserve the precious and rich local folk heritage.

Traditionally, the most important and characteristic manifestations take place on the eve and during the night of the translation. For inhabitants of the Marche province, the evening of December 9 is that of the "Coming," when we remember the miraculous translation by angels of the three intact walls of the Holy House of Nazareth to Loreto hill.

Popular celebrations for the coming of the Holy House began spontaneously and almost immediately since the fourteenth century.[58] However, they were formalized and organized in the seventeenth century mostly in thanks to the preaching and work of Capuchin Fathers Boniface of Ascoli and Thomas of Ancona. In 1624, the municipality of Recanati, to which Loreto then belonged, ordered that on the evening of December 9, "with the shooting of mortars and the sound of all bells, fires are lit over the land of the municipality and lights placed on all city windows and fires lit by peasants throughout the countryside."[59] This gave rise to the tradition of the "fires" (called "*focaracci*" in the Macerata and Fermo areas, "*fugarò*" in the Ancona area, and "*fochère*" in the Ascoli area) that are lit in the countryside, church squares, and village districts of the entire region to light the way for the Virgin Mary and the Child Jesus flying in with their house. It is no coincidence that many churches in the Marche region preserve typical sculptural groups, usually in wood, depicting the Holy House in the form of a small church with a little bell tower, and the Virgin and Child above it. This is why, in the region, Our Lady of Loreto is also known as the Madonna of the "*tettarello*"

---

58   See G. Santarelli, *Tradizioni e Leggende Lauretane*, cit., pp. 26 & ff.

59   Cit. in G. Santarelli, *Tradizioni e Leggende Lauretane*, cit., p. 30.

(small roof – "*de li cuppitti*" in the Macerata area), because she is depicted above the roof of the house.

While varying from town to town, neighborhood to neighborhood, and even family to family, in general, the "fires of the Coming" were lit before or after dinner, but of course, always at night. People gathered around the bonfire, recited the Holy Rosary, and sang the Loreto Litanies, then sang Marian songs and hymns of popular devotion. Besides this, at least one light would be placed on the window or windowsill of each house or building. Commendably, various parishes and local communities have recently reinstated these devotions. As tradition once had it, grandparents or parents would tell children the story of the miraculous translation, and it is easy to imagine how it excited their imagination.

The culminating moment generally took place at 3:00 in the morning, the time when the three walls are thought to have landed in the Marche region. At that time, the bells would ring and many family heads would fire several shots from the windows, to welcome the Coming. Then they would go to church to pray or to attend Mass, which was often celebrated.

CHAPTER III

Where Was Our Lady Born?

Let us now concentrate on another striking event that took place in the Holy House, in addition to the fundamental one, the Annunciation.

Is the home of Nazareth, now in Loreto, also the place where Our Lady was born? Indeed, September 8, Feast of the Nativity of Mary Most Holy, is solemnly celebrated in the sanctuary. Several Pontiffs (for example, Popes Julius II in 1507, Pius IV in 1560, Sixtus V in 1586, and Clement VIII, in 1595), and the Sacred Congregation of Rites, in 1916, granted special indulgences and privileges for that day and confirmed in writing that the dawn of Redemption, the birth of the Mother of God, arose among those three holy walls. Some popes, including Blessed Pius IX, went so far as to write that the Immaculate Conception of the Virgin Mary also took place there (Bull *Inter omnia*, 1852).

Obviously, it is licit to discuss and have a different opinion about this question. No one has absolute certainty about it, nor is it required for salvation. However, we may say that God wrapped certain events in mystery to help us better understand our smallness and stimulate us to investigate and occupy ourselves with "heavenly things," lifting our gaze from the earthly.

However, we cannot ignore some unequivocal facts that would confirm the tradition.

Many Fathers of antiquity, including Epiphanius, Sinazarius Armenus, Hyppolite of Thebes, and above all Western ones have always agreed with the so-called "Nazareth Thesis," which has met increasing consensus over time, from the Middle Ages onward. Suffice it to mention Father Johann von Würtzburg, who cites Pseudo-Jerome: "She was born in Nazareth and in the very same room where, after the angel's salutation, she conceived by the work of the Holy Spirit."[60]

In effect, in the story of the Annunciation and Visitation, Luke suggests that Mary was from Nazareth, where she had her home. After telling the story of Mary's visit to Saint Elizabeth, the Evangelist writes, "And Mary abode with her about three months; and she returned to her own house" (Luke 1:56). And since the Annunciation and Incarnation took place in that house, it is normal to believe that it was later chosen as the home of the Holy Family.

Moreover, several private revelations, such as those to the venerable Mary of Agreda and Blessed Catherine Emmerich, confirm that the Holy Virgin was born in Nazareth. After the miraculous translation of the Holy Halls to Trsat, Our Lady appeared to a local

---

60   Cit. in G. Gorel, *La santa Casa di Loreto*, cit., pp. 31-32.

priest, Fr. Alessandro Giorgiewich, cured him of dropsy and explained that in this house, she was born, grew up, and the Word became flesh.

Our Lady gave the same information in Italy, where she appeared to a hermit in Montorso (Loreto). Moreover, in the fifteenth century, both authors, Teramano and Mantovano, say for certain that Mary's birth took place in the Nazareth house.

In 1578, in a booklet that Pope Gregory XIII ordered translated into eight languages, Teramano wrote, "The Blessed Virgin Mary lived in this room. Here she was born, educated, then greeted by the Angel Gabriel, and shadowed by the Holy Spirit." For his part, Mantovano wrote, "The Temple of the Blessed Mother of Loreto was the very cradle of the Virgin, in which she was born, grew up, was greeted by the Angel Gabriel, and overshadowed by the Holy Spirit."[61]

Teramano and Riera also wrote about the miracle of the flames, a noteworthy miraculous event seen as a divine confirmation of western tradition.[62]

Teramano recalls that before nightfall on September 8, 1460, a local hermit, Paolo della Selva, saw a light from the sky descending toward the Holy House and spreading around the sanctuary. Torsellini recounts that the same phenomenon occurred in 1550 while a Jesuit priest was preaching in the Basilica: Rays of clear light descended over the Holy House, stopped there for some time, and then spread over the crowd present there, finally returning to the sky and vanishing. Father Riera, a historian, was an eyewitness of the event. Two years later, the miracle of the flames was repeated: a

---

61   For both quotations, cf. G. Gorel, *La santa Casa di Loreto*, cit., pp. 222-223.

62   Cf. G. Gorel, *La santa Casa di Loreto*, cit., pp. 155-156.

sort of comet appeared on the inner top of the dome, rested on the Holy House, spread once again over the faithful, and disappeared after pausing above the crucifix present in the Holy House. In 1554, the phenomenon took place outside and was seen also in neighboring towns near Loreto from two in the morning until dawn. Many other such cases have been recorded. In 1389, following these miracles, Pope Urban VI granted the sanctuary a plenary indulgence for September 8. A six-pointed star was hung on the dome in memory of these events. Until the year 1972, on every December 9 (anniversary of the translation, and not for the feast of the Nativity of Mary), the star was lit for the great joy of the faithful, and especially the little ones.[63]

Finally, another truly significant miracle should be noted. In 1654, a converse brother of the order of Saint Francis entered the Holy House of Loreto with a rather skeptical mind towards everything that was said about it. As soon as he crossed the threshold, he immediately fell to the ground as if struck by an illness and even seemed close to death. He was taken out and tended to. When he came to his senses, he cried out in tears: "Yes, this is the birthplace of the Blessed Virgin Mary; this is the sanctuary where the Word was conceived." What happened? What made him change his mind so radically and dispelled all his doubts? He explained that he saw the Mother of God with the Child Jesus looking at him with an irritated air and threatening him with the fire of hell. Struck by a healthy fear, he worked for the rest of his life to proclaim the truth about the Holy House venerated in Loreto.[64]

63 Cf. G. Santarelli, *Tradizioni e Leggende Lauretane*, cit., pp. 55 & ff.

64 Cf. A.R. Caillaux, *Histoire critique et religieuse de Notre Dame de Lorette*, Paris 1843, p. 243.

CHAPTER IV

The Church Has No Doubts

As already mentioned, in 1993 Pope John Paul II called the Holy House of Loreto "the first international sanctuary dedicated to the Virgin and, for several centuries, the true Marian heart of Christianity." He also recalled how it was always the object of special attention on the part of Roman Pontiffs, who made it a frequent pilgrimage destination and object of their apostolic care.

Over the centuries, no less than the popes attest to the importance and extraordinary nature of the Loreto Basilica and the miracle that took place in the Holy House. They have done so with various pronouncements and above all with the liturgy, through which both the authenticity of the Holy House and its miraculous translations have been officially recognized.

4.1 The Feast of the Translation of the Holy House

First of all, we must emphasize that the liturgical feast that occurs on December 10 is that of the "Miraculous Translation" of the Holy House of Nazareth to Loreto, and not the feast of "Our Lady of Loreto," as has been erroneously written in calendars for several years out of ignorance.[65] It is certainly also a Marian feast, and one should bear in mind that in the traditional liturgical calendar, before the reforms of the Second

---

65 Cf. G. Nicolini, *La veridicità storica della miracolosa traslazione della Santa Casa di Nazareth a Loreto* cit., p. 36.

Vatican Council, the formulas of the Mass for that day were the same as those for the dedication of a church, precisely because the Holy House was, and should still be, at the center of the celebration.

The Church has strongly stood behind the establishment of this feast, as the principle *lex orandi, lex credendi* is always valid. And although the miracle of Loreto is not an infallible dogma, like private revelations and many other questions, it is nevertheless true that the pronouncements of the Church about it have been of the utmost authority and deserve respect and obedience.

The institution of this feast, always at the local level, took place under the pontificate of Pope Urban VIII, with a decree of the Congregation of Rites on November 29, 1632, which issued an approval limited to the Marche region.

On August 30, 1669, Pope Clemente IX inserted it into the Roman Martyrology, where it was written: "In Loreto, in the Piceno region, translation of the Holy House of Mary, Mother of God, in which the Word became flesh."[66] The Holy Pontiff himself authorized an office and a Mass for the people of Croatia for the transfer of the Holy House to Trsat. On September 16, 1699, Pope Innocent XII approved a dedicated Office and Mass,[67] and had the story of the prodigy added to the 6th Lesson of the Roman Breviary, which stated: "The house in which the Blessed Virgin Mary was born, consecrated

---

66 Cit. in G. Nicolini, *La veridicità storica della miracolosa traslazione della Santa Casa di Nazareth a Loreto* cit., p. 38.

67 Here is the translation of the prayer then said at Mass: "O Lord, who in your mercy, with the mystery of your Incarnation, sanctified the house of the Blessed Virgin Mary and miraculously carried it into the bosom of your Church, grant that, removed from the house of sinners, we may become worthy inhabitants of your holy tabernacles." Cit. in G. Gorel, *La santa Casa di Loreto*, cit., p. 182 (our translation).

by divine mysteries, was transported through ministry of angels from the land of pagans under the pontificate of St. Celestine V, first to Croatia, then to the territory of Loreto, in the Piceno province. That it is the real house in which the Word became flesh and dwelt among us is proved both by papal letters and bulls, by its well-known veneration throughout the world, and by the continuous miracles obtained here." [68] In this regard, Pope Benedict XIV affirmed that, "wishing to demonstrate the truth of the facts mentioned in this Lesson would be wishing to redo what the historians of the Holy House have done with so much zeal and doctrine."[69]

Pope Benedict XIII and his successors extended the feast to Tuscany, Rome, the Republic of Venice, and then to the entire Italian peninsula and to all nations, dioceses, and religious orders that requested it.

In a decree dated April 16, 1969, the Sacred Congregation of Rites confirmed it once and for all: "It is truly the birthplace of the Blessed Virgin Mary, in which so many divine mysteries were fulfilled. This house so favored, transported by the angels from Palestine to Croatia and then to Loreto, in the Piceno region, manifests itself to everyone with the continual brilliance of its miracles and the constant favor of heavenly gifts: here the Word truly became flesh."[70]

Sometimes, the feast was made obligatory for the whole Church, and other times only at the local level. Until 1956, it was celebrated throughout Italy on December 10, with a double-class rite of the first octave (established by Pope Leo XIII in a brief of July 23, 1894). After 1956, in the context of a simplification of

68 Cit. in *ivi*.

69 Cit. in G. Gorel, *La santa Casa di Loreto*, cit., p. 182.

70 Cit. in *ibidem*, p. 186.

the Missal, the octave disappeared. Then, on February 14, 1961, the Sacred Congregation of Rites issued an instruction establishing that the Translation of the Holy House of the Blessed Virgin Mary should again be celebrated only in the Marche region, as still happens today.

4.2 The Loreto Litanies

One must not leave out, besides the liturgy, the Litany of Loreto, the diffusion of which highlights very well the importance that the sanctuary of Loreto has always had. They were invocations based on pre-existing texts, which the pilgrims recited in the Holy House, and soon became solemnly recognized by the Holy See. The oldest collection of these litanies dates back to the sixteenth century. The first pope to approve them and attach indulgences to them was the Marche-born Franciscan, Pope Sixtus V, with the bull *Reddituri* of July 11, 1587. However, the Holy Office established their current form during the pontificate of Clement VIII, with the decree *Quoniam multi* of September 6, 1601:

"Whereas many private people are spreading new litanies every day on the pretext of fostering devotion; that there is already a great variety of almost countless litanies, in some of which improper phrases have been found, while others, far more seriously, contain dangerous statements that smack of error, seeking with pastoral solicitude to increase devotion and the invocation of God and the Saints among without the danger of spiritual detriment, [Clement VIII] establishes and commands that the faithful stick to the most ancient and common Litanies, which are found in the Breviaries, Missals, Pontificals and Rituals, as well as the Litanies usually sung in the holy temple of Loreto. Anyone who sought to publish other Litanies or use already published ones in churches - both oratories and processions - are required to present them to the Congregation of the Sacred Rites so they may be approved and corrected, if necessary. Let them not try to divulge or recite them in public without the permission and approval of the said Congregation, under severe penalty (in addition to that of the sin committed) inflicted at the discretion of the Ordinary and Inquisitor."[71] For this reason, from then on, every modification and addition to the Loreto Litanies must be approved by the Holy See.

It is interesting to recall that during a trip to Loreto in the summer of 1770, the young Wolfgang Amadeus Mozart was so impressed and entranced by the Holy House that the following year he composed his *Litaniae Lauretanae Beatae Mariae Virginis*.

4.3   The Voice of the Supreme Pontiffs

The popes' pronouncements on Loreto are numerous. It is appropriate that, although briefly, we try to provide a picture as complete as possible.

First, as reported by St. Peter Canisius,[72] it seems that the Marches-born Pope Nicholas IV was aware of the miraculous translation to Trsat. For his part, Boniface VIII was informed of the arrival of the precious relic in Italy. Some argue that the announcement of the first Jubilee of the translation in 1300, only four years after the last transfer of the Holy House, was motivated by the desire to allow Rome-bound pilgrims to go also to Loreto.[73]

The bull of Clement V of July 18, 1310, contains a first, though indirect, explicit reference to the "miracle

---

71   Cit. in A. M. Apollonio, *Le Litanie Lauretane*, Casa Mariana Editrice, Frigento (AV) 2013, p. 7.

72   Cf. G. Santarelli, *La Santa Casa di Loreto*, cit., p. 17.

73   Cf. P.V. Martorelli, *Teatro istorico della Santa Casa*, cit., c. III, p. 50.

of the Holy House." In it, he ratified the vow which some German pilgrims made in Loreto and mentioned the "miraculous divine *Virgo Lauretana*." In 1320, John XXII made other references to the Holy House. Benedict XII granted privileges and indulgences to those who go to pray in Loreto, a decision subsequently confirmed by Urban VI, Boniface IX, Martin V, and Eugene IV. Pope Nicholas V went on pilgrimage to the Holy House twice and ordered that the offered gifts be kept to constitute its treasure.

In 1367, Pope Urban V made an important gesture to confirm the tradition of miraculous translations by sending a statue of the Loreto Virgin to the faithful of Trsat to console them for the sorrow of having lost the Holy House. The Trsatians always considered the appearance of the house a true miracle, and once they learned of its move to Loreto, they began making pilgrimages to that town, asking the Virgin to return and live among them. Even today, that statue of the Virgin of Loreto sent by Urban V is much revered in Trsat and among Slovenians.

Pius II and Paul II had a special relationship with Loreto. Due to a special grace of the *Virgo Lauretana*, Pius II was able to visit the sanctuary even though he was at the end of his life. He died shortly afterward, in 1464 in Ancona, the port city from which departed the Crusade he promoted against the Turks. In 1470, Paul II called an extraordinary Jubilee, limited to the visit to the Basilica, and in the bulls dedicated to it, he spoke of a "miraculously founded" shrine and of a statue of Our Lady which, through admirable divine clemency, arrived with a heavenly escort. When still a cardinal (his name was Pietro Barbo), he assisted Pius II in his illness, and was struck by the plague. As he prayed within the walls of the Holy House, Our Lady appeared, healed him, and foretold his imminent election to the papal throne. That happened on the first scrutiny of the conclave, on August 30, 1464. To show his gratitude and explicitly attest to the miracle, Paul II dedicated his first encyclical to the Virgin of Loreto. The Governor of the Holy House, Vincenzo Casali, had a summary of the document carved on a large marble slab still in the column of the left aisle of the Sanctuary.[74]

Sixtus IV declared Loreto property of the Holy See and conferred on the Holy House the title of *Alma Domus*. On October 21, 1507, Julius II issued a bull confirming the indulgences granted by his predecessors and the miraculous translations, first to Croatia, and then to Italy. He was miraculously honored by the *Virgo Lauretana*, who saved his life during the battle of Mirandola. In 1510, the pope visited the sanctuary, celebrating Mass there on the day of the Nativity of Mary. He also donated, as an *ex-voto,* the cannonball from which he had been saved. Referring to the illustrious relic, Pope Julius II wrote among other things that, "not only is the statue of the Blessed Virgin found in this church, but also, *ut pie creditur et fama est* [as piously believed and reported] according to tradition, here is the room where the Blessed Virgin Mary was conceived, grew up, was greeted by the Angel, conceived the Savior of the world by the power of the Holy Spirit, nourished and raised her divine Son, was enraptured in heavenly things and prayed, and the apostles turned this room into a chapel dedicated to the Blessed Virgin, where the first Mass was celebrated."[75]

---

74 Cf. G. Nicolini, "L'approvazione dei Sommi Pontefici delle miracolose traslazioni della Santa Casa di Nazareth a Loreto," in *Il Segno del soprannaturale*, no. 209, November 2005, p. 19.

75 Cit. *ivi.*

In a brief of June 1, 1515, speaking of the Holy House, Leo X wrote, verbatim: "It is proven by witnesses worthy of faith that the Holy Virgin, after having transported through divine omnipotence her image and house from Nazareth to Croatia, then to the forest of Recanati and the camp of two brothers, had it deposed through the ministry of angels on a public road on which it is still found, and where the Most High, through the merits of the Blessed Virgin, continues to work miracles."[76]

Clement VII sent a delegation to Nazareth to confirm the authenticity of the precious relic, and its response was positive. Julius III founded the College of Penitentiaries in Loreto, entrusting it to the Jesuits. In 1560, Pius IV reiterated that the Blessed Virgin was conceived, born, raised, and greeted by the Angel Gabriel in the sacred room, as attested by testimonies worthy of faith. "It was transported with her statue, by the ministry of angels, from the city of Nazareth to the territory of Recanati, in which it remains the object of profound veneration by all Christian nations."[77]

Pius V, who, as we shall see, resorted to the Virgin of Loreto against Islamic danger, had the Holy House reproduced on the *Agnus Dei,* and never showed the slightest doubt about the House's authenticity.

Gregory XIII founded the Illyrian College and had some coins minted with the effigy of the three Holy Walls.

Sixtus V, a Marches-born pope whose statue stands before the sanctuary, had this inscription written on the facade of the Basilica: "*Deiparae domus in qua Verbum caro factum est*" ("House of the Mother of God, in which

---

76 Cit in G. Nicolini, *La veridicità storica della miracolosa Traslazione della Santa Casa di Nazareth a Loreto*, cit., p. 32.

77 Cit. in G. Gorel, *La santa Casa di Loreto*, cit., p. 174.

the Word became flesh"). Sixtus V gave to it the title of city and bishopric, "considering that Loreto enjoys extraordinary worldwide fame because in the center of his church is the holy room in which the Virgin Mary was born, greeted by the Angel, and conceived the Holy Savior of the world; that this room was transported by angels to this place, and that continuous miracles are performed here to the benefit of numerous believers flocking here from all over the world."[78] In 1586, Sixtus V founded the Order of Our Lady of Loreto (Loreto Knights), with the task of defending the city and protecting the Ancona area from raids by corsairs and Turks.

In 1595, Pope Clement VIII, also born in the Marche region, had carved on the marble covering of the Holy House a Latin inscription tracing its origin and miraculous appearance: "Christian pilgrim, coming here by devotion or choice, admire the Holy House of Loreto, venerated throughout the world for its divine mysteries and miracles. Here was born Mary the Most Holy Mother of God; here she was greeted by the Angel, and the eternal Word of God became incarnate. The Angels moved this house from Palestine, first time to Trsat in Croatia, in 1291, under the pontificate of Nicholas IV. Three years later, early in the pontificate of Boniface VIII, through the same angelic ministry, it was transported to a forest in the Piceno region, near the city of Recanati. In the space of a year, it changed places three times, finally establishing itself here for the last 300 years. From that time, as such wonderful novelties moved neighboring peoples, and later this Holy House became greatly venerated among all peoples, as the fame of its miracles became widespread, of which the walls without foundations, remain stable and whole

78 Cit. in G. Gorel, *La santa Casa di Loreto*, cit., pp. 174-175.

after so many centuries. In the year 1534, Clement VII had it surrounded with decorated marble. In the year 1595, Clement VIII P.M. ordered that a brief history of the admirable Translation be inscribed into this marble. Antonio M. Cardinal Gallo, Bishop of Osimo and Protector of the Holy House, had this notice written: You, pious pilgrim, venerate the Queen of Angels and Mother of graces with devotional affection so that, through her merits and prayers, you may obtain from her sweetest Son, the Author of life, forgiveness for your sins, bodily holiness, and the joys of eternity."[79]

Benedict XIV, in his work *On the Feasts of Jesus Christ Our Lord and the Blessed Virgin Mary*, written when he was still cardinal archbishop of Bologna, speaking of the Holy House and drawing, among others, from St. Peter Canisius and the famous historian Cardinal Caesar Baronius, called it, "Abode in which the Divine Word took human flesh, carried by the ministry of angels as attested by ancient documents and perpetual tradition, as well as by testimonies of Supreme Pontiffs, the common sentiment of the faithful, and the miracles that continuously occur." Furthermore, in his monumental work *De Servorum Dei Beatificatione et Beatorum Canonizatione* (book III, chap. X, no. 5), Pope Lambertini wrote:

"...Some have dared to call a fable the translation of the holy house, in which the Word became flesh, moved from Galilee to the Marches region, allegedly because of a lack of contemporary authors who narrate that translation. ... However, permit me to note that contemporary authors did exist, as witnessed by

79   Cit. in G. Nicolini, *Miracolose Traslazioni della Santa Casa di Nazareth a Loreto*, in http://www.vaticano.com/la-traslazione-miracolosa-nella-selva-della-signora-loreta/.

Guido Grandi (cit. dissert. 3 chap. 8 no. 12). He explains that there have been reliable documents from that region since the coming of the holy house to Italy ... which are older than Antonino himself (whose silence the supporters of negationism used in this controversy). No prudent man would tell Antonino that he should have included in his stories an express testimony of a well-known event, and hence it is obvious that some negationist authors intentionally abused his silence to challenge the truth of the house of Loreto. Suffice also to read the Fluminense annals, by Girolamo Angelita, historian of the house of Loreto, who studied and described its whole history, and the testimony of Antonio Salt in his book, *Sanctuarium Lauretanum*, to see that there is no lack of contemporary documents. We must also trust famous writers such as the above-mentioned Angelita, and Orazio Torsellino, who had these writings in their hands when writing the history of Loreto, and drew their narratives from them."

More recently, Pius IX, also born in the Marche region and very devoted to the Virgin of Loreto, was miraculously cured of epilepsy in his youth after making a promise and was able to enter ecclesiastical life. In 1852, in the Bull *Inter omnia*, he wrote that, "among all shrines consecrated to the Immaculate Virgin Mother of God, the venerable and august House of Loreto takes the first place and shines with incomparable brilliance. Consecrated by divine mysteries, illustrated by countless miracles, honored by the influx of peoples, the glory of its name extends to the Universal Church and rightly is an object of veneration to all nations and human lineages. Indeed, in Loreto is venerated that House of Nazareth so dear to the Heart of God, built in Galilee and later ripped from its foundations and transported beyond the seas by divine power, first to Croatia, and then into Italy. Precisely in that House the Blessed Virgin was conceived, perfectly exempt from the original guilt by eternal divine disposition, born and grew, and was greeted by the heavenly messenger as full of grace and blessed among women. Precisely in that House, filled with God, and under the fruitful work of the Holy Spirit, without losing anything of her inviolable virginity, she became the Mother of the Only Begotten Son of God."[80]

On the occasion of the sixth centenary of the miraculous translation, Leo XIII, a great devotee of the Loreto sanctuary, published the Brief *Felix Nazaretana* (January 23, 1894) with words of enthusiasm: "As the chronicles of the Church narrate, this House immediately attracted the pious aspirations and fervent devotion of everyone, keeping them alive for centuries, as soon as it was prodigiously transported to Italy, in the Piceno area by a supreme act of divine benevolence, and opened for worship on the hills of Loreto. ... Let everyone understand — Italians first and foremost — this particular gift of God, Who so providentially took the House from unworthy powers[81] and offered it to them in a significant act of love. In fact, that blessed dwelling marked the beginning of human salvation with the great and prodigious mystery of God made man, who reconciles lost humanity with the Father, and restores all things."[82] It was under the pontificate of Pope Leo XIII that the Universal Congregation of the Holy House (1883) was founded, with the aim of promoting the

---

80   Cit in G. Gorel, *La santa Casa di Loreto*, cit., p. 188. Cf. also G. Nicolini, *La veridicità storica della miracolosa Traslazione della Santa Casa di Nazareth a Loreto*, cit., p. 33.

81   That of the Muslims, who had invaded the Holy Land.

82   Cf. G. Gorel, *La santa Casa di Loreto*, cit., pp. 188-189.

Marian-Loretan veneration and providing for the care of the Basilica.

Under St. Pius X, the Loreto devotion faced the French Canon Ulysses Chevalier's rationalist criticisms, collected in the book *Notre Dame de Lorette – Étude historique sur l'authenticité de la Santa Casa* (1906), in which he casts doubt on the authenticity of the Holy House and its miraculous translations on the pretext of fighting "superstition" and "purifying" the faith. The book received praise (but not an imprimatur) from the Master of the Sacred Palaces, as in his opinion, it did not affect the piety of the faithful. However, the then-Secretary of State, Cardinal Rafael Merry del Val, answering on behalf of the pontiff a question made to the Holy See about the book, replied that, "concerning the recent publication by Canon Chevalier, the statement by the Master of Sacred Palaces was not at all pleasing to His Holiness. In this regard, His Holiness did not hide his displeasure and has instructed me to reveal it to you publicly. From this, you will easily deduce that in this case, the words of the Rev. Master cannot raise any obstacle to further work of research and refutation."[83]

In 1907 the Universal Congregation created a "Perpetual Defense College of the Holy House," to unmask lies about the authenticity of the Holy House and its miraculous translation. Pope Saint Pius X also agreed to finance the Jesuit Father Ilario Rinieri (1853-1941), to study the Loreto question and defend the tradition against Chevalier's attacks. He did so in his famous three-volume work titled *La Santa Casa di Loreto* (Turin 1910-1911).

The times of the pontificate of Pius X saw the appearance of modernism, "the synthesis of all heresies,"

---

83 Cit. in G. Gorel, *La santa Casa di Loreto*, cit., p. 195.

as he defined it in his encyclical *Pascendi* (1907), so it is no wonder that the Loreto tradition was the target of rationalist and skeptical criticisms.

In this regard, it is useful to report the words that Fr. Thomas, WTO, pronounced at the Marian Congress of Le Puy in 1910. With the full approval of Pius X, he noted that behind the controversy about Loreto, "we must recognize there is a clash of a hypercritical mentality very close to Modernism, from which even the best can hardly defend themselves. ... Let people with a healthy critical mind judge it: On the one hand you have a school born yesterday that seeks to reform conclusions issued with full knowledge of the facts ... and makes biased judgments; on the other, you have the top scholars of the Catholic world, the Roman Pontiffs, saints, the Christian people in their catholicity, recognized authentic documents, and conclusions of official Commissions. Bona fide people cannot hesitate. The truth is certainly not found in a few isolated units that have distorted history. ... Protestantism in the seventeenth century, philosophism in the eighteenth, rationalism in the nineteenth, hypercriticism in the twentieth century will not be able to hide the truth of the historical fact. The relic is certainly authentic: the true science bows, and the faith of the Christian people remains unchanged. The Roman Pontiffs unceasingly proclaimed the truth, and the tradition remains constant. The Holy House is precisely the House in which the Word became flesh."[84]

Pope Benedict XV confirmed the miraculous transport of the holy walls in an even more solemn and definitive way, when he declared the Blessed Virgin of Loreto "Patroness of aviators and all air travelers" on March 24, 1920. This was due precisely to the recognition of the

---

84   Cit. in G. Gorel, *op.cit.*, pp. 202-204.

historical authenticity of the "miraculous flight" of the Holy House. [85]

Pius XI blessed a statue of Our Lady of Loreto that accompanied Umberto Nobile[86] on a mission to the North Pole and chose Loreto for the Italian National Eucharistic Congress of 1930. The Holy See, by virtue of the Lateran Treaty, also regained control of the Basilica and its assets. Of note in this regard is the address that Cardinal Granito Pignatelli di Belmonte addressed to Pope Pius XI on the occasion of the new year (1935) on behalf of the Sacred College. Among the topics, the Cardinal also had a thought for Loreto: "We do not want to pass over in silence the great gesture with which Your Holiness was pleased to give a new constitution to one of the dearest treasures Christianity possesses in our Italy, the Holy House of Loreto. Could there be a more venerated Marian shrine than the House consecrated by the personal presence of Mary, in which she lived her mortal life, this 'little

85 Attesting to the popularity of this provision and the spread of devotion, suffice it to recall, by way of example, that the poet Gabriele D'Annunzio himself dealt with Loreto several times in his literary works, although his ideas and conduct were not strictly pro-Catholic. On December 10, 1937, he wrote to General Valle: "Today, December 10, is the Translation of the Holy House of Loreto, which in the first ardor of the war I proposed (sic!) to be recognized by aviators and declared as the Protectress of Aviators in war and peace. I am certain that all my faithful companions honor the Winged Virgin, '*in Dalmatiam prius, deinde in Agrum Lauretanum translata fuit*' [who was first transferred to Croatia, and then to the field of Loreto] ... Today, I dare to remind you of this miraculous date so that you may call our Aviators to gaze at the waters of our Adriatic, which perpetually radiate so much votive glory." American astronaut James McDivitt and his two companions took with them a blessed medal with the effigy of Our Lady of Loreto in the Apollo 9 flight of March 3-13, 1969. For these and other information, cf. "80° Anniversario della proclamazione della Madonna di Loreto a Patrona dell'Aviazione, taken from *Il Messaggio della Santa Casa*, no. 7, July-August 2000.

86 Umberto Nobile (1885-1978), one of the leading exponents of the Italian air force, became famous throughout the world for his two flights (in 1926 and 1928) to the North Pole in an airship.

On October 4, 1962, Pope John XXIII went to the sanctuary as a pilgrim to ask for protection for the Church because of the imminent opening of the Second Vatican Council.

Pope Saint John Paul II, who went to the sanctuary five times, and Pope Benedict XVI, on two occasions.

treasure' that witnessed the ineffable scene of the Annunciation, in which, with her *'Fiat,'* Mary agreed to become the Co-Redemptrix of the human race by welcoming the Divine Word into her most pure bosom? That is why, Holy Father, just as no sincere Christian can be found who does not tenderly love the Blessed Virgin, so also no Christian fails to rejoice and exult at the sight of the Holy House, an object of your papal care and solicitude."[87]

Pius XII granted priests the privilege of being able to celebrate the Holy Sacrifice of the Mass on the altar of the Holy House for twenty-four consecutive hours on March 25, Feast of the Annunciation.

Addressing faithful from the Marches region residing in Rome on March 23, 1958, Pope Pius XII earnestly mentioned the Loreto sanctuary, which he had defined in a 1956 speech as "distinguished and dear."[88] "As for your characteristic spiritual values, suffice to think of the Holy House of Loreto to see a very special blessing of Mary, who has brought and brings you visits of innumerable souls, who come to you bringing an attitude of sincere piety, ardent faith, profound humility, and a spirit of mortification proper to every truly devout pilgrimage."[89]

John XXIII went to the sanctuary as a pilgrim on October 4, 1962, to ask protection for the Church because of the imminent opening of the Second Vatican Council. On that occasion, in addition to recalling the

---

87 Cit. In G. Gorel, *La santa Casa di Loreto*, cit., p. 210.

88 Cf. *Radiomessaggio di Sua Santità Pio XII alle partecipanti al pellegrinaggio nazionale al santuario della Vergine Ssma. di Loreto*, in https://w2.vatican.va/content/pius-xii/it/speeches/1956/documents/hf_p-xii_spe_19561014_pellegrinaggio-loreto.html.

89 Pius XII, *Discorso ai marchigiani residenti in Roma*, March 23, 1958, in https://w2.vatican.va/content/pius-xii/it/speeches/1958/documents/hf_p-xii_spe_19580323_marchigiani.html.

visits he made before becoming Supreme Pontiff, the pope retraced the centuries-old devotion of so many souls and many of his predecessors: "Religious piety moved popes and illustrious personalities of every century to pause in prayer in this Basilica of Loreto, which extends over the slope of the Piceni hills towards the Adriatic Sea. Animated by fervent faith in God and by veneration for the Mother of Jesus and our own, they came here on pilgrimage, sometimes in times of difficulties and grave anxieties for the Church. Suffice it to recall, among others, Popes Pius II, Paul III, the initiator of the Council of Trent, Pius VI, and Pius VII, Gregory XVI, and Pius IX, and also St. Charles Borromeo, St. Francis of Sales, and other saints and Blessed, to have a portion of edifying encouragement."[90]

Many of the recent popes visited Loreto as well. We have already mentioned John Paul II, who went to the sanctuary five times. Until now, Benedict XVI was the last one to have visited it, on two occasions. On September 2, 2007, speaking to the residents of Loreto, he recommended that they never forget the "great privilege of living in the shadow of the Holy House."[91]

Referring to the Holy House during a homily on October 4, 2012, he emphasized that "this humble abode is a concrete and tangible testimony of the greatest event in our history: the Incarnation; the Word became flesh, and Mary, the servant of the Lord, is the privileged channel through which God came to dwell among us." He went on to point out that, "it [the House] was placed on a road, which

---

90   Cit. in G. Gorel, *La santa Casa di Loreto*, cit., p. 216b.

91   Benedict XVI, *Encounter with the Faithful of Loreto*, September 2, 2007 at https://w2.vatican.va/content/benedict-xvi/it/speeches/2007/september/documents/hf_ben-xvi_spe_20070902_fedeli-loreto.html.

might seem rather strange; from our point of view, house and street seem to exclude each other. In reality, this particular aspect contains a singular message from this House. It is not a private house belonging to a person or a family, but a dwelling open to everyone, which is, so to speak, on all of our paths. Here in Loreto, we find a house that makes us stay, live, and at the same time walk, reminding us that we are all pilgrims who must always be on the way to another house, the final home, the eternal city, the abode of God with redeemed humanity."[92]

As for its juridical structure, the Sanctuary of the Holy House has been directly subject to the Apostolic See since 1507. Until 1698, it was run by a cardinal protector and then by the Loreto Congregation, presided over by the Cardinal Secretary of State represented in Loreto by a prelate-governor. The sanctuary always enjoyed a special legal status even during the various political upheavals that took place from the French invasion in 1797 to the Savoy occupation in 1860. After the Concordat between the Holy See and Italy in 1929, its governance was entrusted to the Administration of the Pontifical Basilica of the Holy House, governed by a Pontifical Administrator appointed directly by the Holy See and represented in Loreto by a Vicar, who received the episcopal dignity (see bull *Lauretanae Basilicae*, of September 15, 1934).

On June 24, 1965, with the Constitution *Lauretanae Almae Domus*, Paul VI suppressed the Pontifical Administration of the Basilica and established the Pontifical Delegation for the Sanctuary of the Holy

---

92 Benedict XVI, *Homily on the Pastoral Visit to Loreto*, October 4, 2012, at *https://w2.vatican.va/content/benedict-xvi/it/homilies/2012/documents/hf_ben-xvi_hom_20121004_loreto.html.*

St. Nicholas of Tolentino learned supernaturally of the Holy House's flight at three in the morning between December 9 and 10, 1294, while in prayer. According to accounts, upon the sacred abode's arrival on Italian soil, bells began to ring by themselves in celebration, and many trees bent toward the House as a sign of homage.

House of Loreto. He also established the Prelature of the Holy House with canonical jurisdiction over the municipal territory of Loreto, and elevated the Basilica of the Holy House to the status of a cathedral, designating the Papal Delegate to govern it as Prelate.

4.4 The Presence of Saints

It would require a separate work to provide a list of all the saints who visited the Holy House and spoke about it. [93]

Here we limit ourselves to some particularly significant examples, useful to understand that the saints always firmly believed both in the authenticity of the Holy House and in its miraculous translation.

Saint Francis of Assisi[94] is said to have prophesied the arrival of the Holy House in the Marche region in 1215, when he received from the municipality of Sirolo a convent for his friars. While visiting the building, the great saint looked at the valley and forest from a distance and predicted the miraculous coming of the precious relic (the artist Cesare Maccari depicted this episode in one of the four-walled segments of the small arches of the sanctuary dome).

While in prayer at three in the morning between December 9 and 10, 1294, Saint Nicholas of Tolentine[95] was informed by supernatural means of the flight of the Holy House. According to the accounts from the time, when the sacred residence arrived in Italian soil, the bells began to ring by themselves, [96] and many trees bent toward it as a sign of homage, albeit the wind was blowing in the opposite direction. Maccari painted this episode in one of the segments already mentioned.

---

93 For an overall view, see M. Montanari-A. Schiaroli, *Santi e beati a Loreto*, Congregazione Universale Santa Casa, Loreto 2005.

94 Cf. G. Santarelli, *Tradizioni e Leggende Lauretane*, cit., pp. 144 & ff.

95 Cf. *ibidem*, pp. 147 & ff.

96 A similar phenomenon, with heavenly music heard by the inhabitants, happened in 1467 in Genazzano, near Rome, when the image of Our Lady of Good Counsel miraculously arrived there, transported to Italy from Scutari (Albania) to escape the Islamic invasion.

Saint Catherine of Bologna, whose body is still incorrupt and miraculously seated (when her body was exhumed, responding to an order of her superior, the saint moved on her own and placed herself in the position where she can still be seen, totally inexplicable from a scientific point of view), told of a revelation she received from Jesus about the miraculous translation of the Holy House. On March 25, 1440, Jesus spoke to her about the Holy House and said, "Due to the idolatry of those people [the Turks who had occupied Palestine] it was transported to Croatia by a host of angels. For the same reasons and others, they brought this worthy church to various places. Finally, the holy angels placed it permanently in Loreto, in the province of Italy, and the lands of Holy Church." Saint Catherine of Bologna was a cloistered nun[97], had never been to Loreto, and therefore, could not have read the story on the plaque placed in the sanctuary about the miraculous translation occurring "to various places," as this was handed down by different local traditions, and not written in any known document at the time. Mystical phenomena must certainly be taken with caution but cannot be considered as mere inventions or fantasies.

The case of Blessed Anne Catherine Emmerich is equally significant, for two reasons. First, thanks to her mystical experiences, she was able to identify the house in Ephesus where Mary Most Holy likely lived the last years of her earthly existence. Second, her life was a continuous miracle. Immobilized in bed for a disease, and bearing the stigmata, she fed exclusively on the Eucharist in her last 11 years. Without ever having seen the Holy House, she was able to describe

---

97   Cit. in G. Nicolini, La veridicità storica della miracolosa traslazione della Santa Casa di Nazareth a Loreto, cit., p. 18.

it exactly, declaring that the Annunciation had taken place there and that its walls were absolutely the same as in Nazareth. She also had a vision of the miraculous translation: "I have often seen, in vision, the translation of the Holy House of Loreto. ... I saw the Holy House transported over the sea by seven angels. It had no foundation. ... Three angels held it from one side and three from the other; the seventh hovered in front, with a long trail of light above him..."[98]

We cannot forget the famous vision that St. Joseph of Cupertino had when he came to Osimo, a city a few miles from Loreto, where he lived the last part of his life. He saw innumerable ranks of angels rising from and descending to the sanctuary of the Holy House, bearing witness to the sacredness of that place and the relic kept there. During this vision, he too rose up in an ecstatic flight, as had happened to him countless times before thousands of witnesses, for which he was called "the saint of flights." That mystical flight at the sight of the Basilica of the Holy House, witnessed by many at the event, became a direct "confirmation" of the authenticity of the "miraculous flight" of the Holy House, operated by divine omnipotence.

Even the stigmatized Saint Veronica Giuliani received extraordinary graces during two mystical pilgrimages to the Holy House of Loreto, on December 10, 1714, and December 10, 1715, feast of the Miraculous Translation. Her confessor, Jesuit Father Mario Cursoni, gave her this disconcerting command: "After you receive Communion, you and I will go to Loreto to visit Mary Most Holy." Thus, having received Eucharistic communion, after a rapture of the spirit, she

---

98 Cit. in G. Nicolini, La veridicità storica della miracolosa traslazione della Santa Casa di Nazareth a Loreto, cit., p. 21.

began her mystical pilgrimage to Loreto. In her diary, the saint noted, "As if flying, I found myself in Loreto, in the Church of Mary Most Holy. It was a large church, and inside it was, after the high altar, a smaller church. So it seemed to me." In the Proceedings of her beatification and canonization process, her confessor, Father Cursoni, stated that Veronica, whom he had questioned in this regard, described the Sanctuary so well and in such detail that he could not have done better if he had been there several times. This is why he asked her if she had ever been to Loreto before entering the cloister, and she assured him that she had never been there. On December 10, 1714, the saint wrote, "I remained entirely to Mary in everything." The Virgin, present in the Holy House, assured her that she was "the mediatrix between God and creatures," and that all graces pass through her hands.

Visitors to Loreto, among others, were St. Charles Borromeo, St. Francis de Sales in his youth, and St. Francis Xavier, who received there the inspiration to leave for India and Japan, and healed several Orientals simply by having them touch the Loreto Litanies he had written. In Loreto, he healed St. Francis Borgia. St. Louis Maria Grignion de Montfort stayed there for two whole weeks and received the inspiration to write his famous *Treatise of True Devotion to Mary*. Montfort was a great devotee of the Holy House of Loreto. Precisely because of the extraordinary fact that occurred there – the Incarnation of God in the bosom of the Blessed Virgin Mary – we can say that the Loreto sanctuary is the ideal place for all those who practice the slavery of love to the Blessed Mother. Yes, Loreto is also the House of the slaves of Mary, according to the method the great French saint teaches in his *Treatise*. It is no coincidence that he recommends holding special celebrations on March 25, the day of the Annunciation, because it is the day on which Our Lord Jesus Christ himself became the slave of Our Lady.

Saint Benedict Joseph Labre came every year from 1775 to 1783. Saint Alphonsus Maria de Liguori spoke of Loreto in his *Glories of Mary*, defending the truth of the miraculous translations and the authenticity of the Holy House. [99] Also, Saint Stanislaus Kostka, Saint Louis Gonzaga, and Saint John Berchmans went on pilgrimage to the Marian shrine.

How can we forget the emotion felt by Saint Therese of the Child Jesus when, as a young girl, she came to the sanctuary with her family? So it was with many other saints and blessed pilgrims to Loreto and the Holy House, who received extraordinary graces and also an inspiration to establish religious Orders and Congregations.

We conclude this chapter with a few words of St. Peter Canisius, who tenaciously fought against the lies of Lutherans, the first who systematically questioned

---

99 In his Christmas Novena, the saint wrote, "O fortunate little house of Nazareth, I salute and venerate you. A time will come when you will be visited by the leading men of the earth; pilgrims visiting you will not cease to cry out with tenderness thinking that the King of paradise was brought up within your poor walls for almost his entire life. In this house, the Incarnate Word lived for the rest of his childhood and youth. How did he live? He lived in poverty, despised by men as a mere apprentice carpenter and obeying Mary and Joseph ... Oh God, how tender it is to think that the Son of God lived like a servant in this poor house! Now he goes to fetch water, now he opens or closes the shop, now cleans the room or he picks up pieces of wood for the fire, now struggles to help Joseph in his work. O Wonder! see a God who cleans up, a God who serves as a waiter! Oh how we should all be burning with holy love for this Redeemer reduced to such baseness to be loved by us! We adore above all the hidden and neglected life that Jesus Christ lived in the house of Nazareth. O proud men, how can you aspire to show off and be honored, seeing your God spend thirty years of his life living in poverty, hidden and unknown, to teach us how to lead a humble and hidden life?" Cit. in T. Rey-Mermet, *The Saint of the Age of Enlightenment*, Città Nuova, Florence 1983, pp. 634-635.

the authenticity of the Holy House. In his work, *De Maria Virgine Libri quinque* (1577), in the section dedicated to Our Lady of Loreto, he writes: "In Loreto, the miracle manifested itself with such power, fame, constancy, evidence, and prodigality that all of Europe was astonished and that no one but a daredevil could escape from the omnipotent hand of the Most High, to which all these manifest signs constitute as many public testimonies to the whole world, besides all the other proofs, to the truth of the marvelous translation of the Holy House of Nazareth." [100]

100 Cit. in G. Gorel, *La santa Casa di Loreto*, cit., p. 161.

CHAPTER V

Loreto, a Bulwark of Christian Europe against Islam

Among the innumerable historical facts related to it, the sanctuary of Loreto played a vital role in the struggle of Christianity against Islamic aggression. When facing attacks from the Muslim world, Catholic peoples invoked the Virgin of Loreto to protect the Papacy, the Catholic Church, and European Christian identity in general.

To have an idea of the importance of Loreto, suffice it to mention two momentous events, decisive for the history of relations between our continent and Islam: the battles of Lepanto and Vienna.

5.1 The Battle of Lepanto (1571)

The battle of Lepanto held back Turkish expansionism towards the West. In addition to the heroism of those who fought and shed their blood, the Christian armies won the victory due to an intervention of Our Lady, invoked precisely as *Virgo Lauretana*. It is no coincidence, therefore, that at the end of the naval conflict, some war trophies were donated to the sanctuary, such as flags, banners, and weapons taken from the Turkish enemy.

If the Christians had been defeated, Islam would have spread to Europe and taken possession of our lands, subjugating us by imposing its religion and political domination.

Let us hear Father Arsenio D'Ascoli, who in his work *The Popes and the Holy House*[101] has delved into those events in more detail.

"Saint Pius V placed under the protection of the Virgin of Loreto the outcome of the great battle that Christian nations were fighting against the Turks, who were making a final effort by sea to break through the Western Mediterranean and strike at the heart of the Catholic Church. The Holy Pontiff had ordered continuous prayers in the Holy House of Loreto throughout the period of the last great crusade.

"While the military glory for the battle of Lepanto shines on the legendary figure of Don John of Austria, the victory resulted only from the confident prayer of St. Pius V. Out of love for the Church in danger, he who hated war so spoke to the cardinals gathered in Consistory on April 2, 1566: 'I am arming myself against the Turks, but prayer alone can help me with this.' The Pope went barefoot on a procession in the streets of Rome to 'bend' the goodness of God towards his Church; at the same time, however, he prepared weapons and erected lookout towers along the entire coast of the sea of Rome.

"On May 25, 1571, the 'Christian League' was signed in Rome. Mark Anthony Colonna, commander of the pontifical fleet, went to Loreto with his wife to put the fate of war into Mary's hands.

"The Christian fleet sailed from European ports, and after twenty days of navigation, came in sight of the strong enemy fleet, which had 300 ships. Don John of Austria, handsome and with a luminous face like an archangel of victory, went from ship to ship with a crucifix in hand; he infused ardor and courage and hoisted the

---

101   A. D'Ascoli, *I Papi e la Santa Casa*, Loreto, 1969, pp. 54 & ff.

Pope's standard and the flag of the expedition, topped by a statue of the Virgin. It was a prayer sign for all ships.

"That was a particularly solemn moment. Behind them, Europe and the Pope were anxious. The Virgin of Loreto invoked with ardor by her children, took part in the gigantic battle. The furious melee began around noon on October 7, 1571. At five in the evening, the battle was over.

"On that same day, Saint Pius V was working with various prelates going over the finances of the enterprise. All of a sudden, as if moved by an irresistible impulse, he got up, went to the window, stared at the east as if in ecstasy. Then, he turned back to the prelates, his eyes shining with divine joy: 'Let us cease dealing with business,' he exclaimed, 'let us go to thank God. The Christian fleet has won.' He dismissed the prelates and immediately went to the chapel, where a cardinal, who had rushed in on hearing the happy announcement, found him shedding tears of joy.

"However, the official news came with some delay because a storm of sea forced the messenger of Don John of Austria to stop.

"On his arrival (the night of October 21, 1571), the Pope welcomed him, exclaiming, 'The Lord has heeded the prayer of the humble and did not disdain their entreaties. Let these things be handed down to posterity so people to be born will praise the Lord.'

"The pontiff issued a medal engraved with the words of the Psalmist: 'The right hand of the Lord has done great things; this comes from God.' Moving on to the valiant *Generalissimo*, he applied to him the word of the Angel, '*Fuit homo missus a Deo cui nomen erat Joannes.*'[102] In 1863, the

---

102   "There was a man sent from God, whose name was John" (Jn 1:6).

On May 25, 1571, the "Christian League" was signed in Rome. Marco
Antonio Colonna, commander of the papal fleet, came to Loreto with
his wife to place the fate of the war in Mary's hands. And in 1576,
John of Austria came to Loreto to fulfill the vow he had made to Our
Lady five years earlier when he left for the battle of Lepanto.
The decoration of the Great Hall of Palazzo Colonna in Rome
celebrates the role of Marco Antonio in the battle of Lepanto.
Fresco by Giovanni Coli and Filippo Gherardi, 1675-1678.

same thing was done for John Sobieski in Vienna.

"The Pontiff, seized with irrepressible joy, ordered all those who were in bed to get up and come with him to the chapel to glorify the divine goodness.

"The victory of Lepanto is therefore intimately linked to the Sanctuary of Loreto. The special devotion to Our Lady of the Rosary was born and developed from this historic battle, the victory of which was obtained through the visible patronage of the Virgin of Loreto. The invocation 'Help of Christians' was added to the Loreto Litany after this victory, which Saint Pius V also attributed to the Virgin of Loreto. 'Therefore, the really pious Pope,' writes Zucchi, 'initiated private and public prayers to reconcile with the great God. He ordered ardent prayers be continually addressed to Our Lady in her most holy cell of Loreto to help her Christians in great danger and need. The hope of Pope Pius and other pious persons was not in vain.'[103]

"As a memorial, and in gratitude, the Pope had the image of Loreto coined on *Agnus Dei* medallions with these magnificent words: *Vera Domus florida quae fuit in Nazareth.*[104] Under it he inscribed '*Sub tuum praesidium,*' to make everyone understand who should be credited with the victory.

"Here is another telltale fact on the intervention of the Virgin of Loreto in the outcome of the battle. While Marcantonio Colonna, commander of the papal army, left for the East, his wife Felice Orsini went to Loreto with other ladies to pray for her husband and for victory. She spent days and nights in very devout prayer. Seeing her fervor and faith, a young Jew converted and was baptized in the Holy House. Mrs. Orsini acted as his godmother and took him as a squire.

"Rome prepared a triumphal entry for the victorious general of the papal army, but the Christian leader, recognizing that credit for the victory should not go to him but to the Virgin of Loreto, postponed his return to the capital and came to Loreto to thank Our Lady.

---

103   Martorelli, vol. I, p. 531
104   "The true, splendid House that was at Nazareth."

"The whole papal armada moored at Port Recanati. Its commander, officers, and Christians, freed from the Turks, went to Loreto hill on foot, heads uncovered, singing hymns of joy and thanksgiving.[105]

"In 1576, Don John of Austria came to Loreto to fulfill the vow made to Our Lady five years earlier, when he left for the battle of Lepanto. Until then, he had always been hindered by pressing political and military affairs. He came to Loreto from Naples on horseback, in the dead of winter. As soon as he saw the Sanctuary from afar, he stopped, bowed, and uncovered his head in reverence. 'Coming to the blessed Cell, after a general confession, he gave infinite thanks to Our Lady and added to his already fulfilled vow a rich gift of money. Having fulfilled both his vow and pious duty, he returned to Naples with great veneration for that most lovely Lady of Loreto.'[106]

"In Lepanto, the Turkish armada had about 40,000 rowers, a large number of whom were Christians. Fifteen thousand of them were released after the great battle and taken back to Europe on Christian ships.

"It is well known that on the same day before the battle began, the Christian slaves of the Turks chained in the ships to row, had recourse to Our Lady of Loreto to obtain their freedom.[107]

"Everyone then went to Loreto, individually or in groups, to fulfill their promise. 'And as a souvenir of that heavenly favor, they left to their *Liberatrix* the chains that held them tied to the oars.'[108]

"These chains were used to manufacture the gates

---

105   Martorelli, vol. I, pp. 430-431.

106   Ibid, vol. I, pp. 433-434.

107   Ibid, vol. I, p. 431.

108   Ibid, vol. I, 431.

Many of the 40,000 rowers of the Turkish army in Lepanto were Christians. About 15,000 of them were released in the great battle and brought back to Europe on Christian ships. Before the battle began, the Christian slaves chained to row in Turkish ships entrusted themselves to Our Lady of Loreto to obtain their freedom. The four gates of the Holy House, in addition to the chapels' gates, were forged with the chains of slaves who came to Loreto.

to the twelve altars of the central nave of the Basilica, where they remained for almost two centuries. Finally, 'when the marble balustrades were placed at the said chapels, those gates were removed and the iron, mixed indistinctly with others, was used in various factories belonging to the Sanctuary.' [109]

"The four gates of the Holy House and the railings of the chapels were made with the chains of slaves who came to Loreto, still preserved in place as a memento. The great spears were used to make an enclosure around the fountain of Maderno, and with the arrows, they built a railing around a chapel of the Basilica. All eventually rusted, and the chapels were given another style to harmonize with the new altars. However, Sacconi did not

109 Idem, vol. II, p.134.

like these marble balustrades similar to the barriers of theater boxes.[110]

"Where were they taken? Some to basements, others were used for other purposes, still others to the municipal dartboard.

"The gesture of those slaves who donated their chains to their *Liberatrix* as a sign of gratitude and love was really nice. Although they are simple and rough, the four gates of the Holy House are there to sing the glories and victories of the Virgin and to remind all those who are slaves of their passions to break their chains at the feet of Mary and rise up free and pure. ...

"In his dictionary of historical-ecclesiastical scholarship, under the heading 'Ancona,' Moroni categorically states that Pope Saint Pius V took himself to the Doric city in 1566 to order the construction of fortifications against the Turks.[111] Perhaps on that occasion he went to visit the Holy House to which he had shown devotion since he became a cardinal.

"Even the archivist of the Holy House, Pietro Giannuizzi ... says that the Pope visited Loreto in 1566 to implore the Virgin for help and assistance for the Church threatened by the Turks. Only Fr. Diego Calcagni, in the memories of the city of Recanati, states that the Pope visited Loreto after the naval victory and went in procession to the Holy House.

"He also sent a pallium and a magnificent chasuble to the Basilica through Cardinal Michele Monelli, who went to Loreto to thank Our Lady for his recovery."[112]

---

110   Cf. Vogel, Index Hist. 10-5-75.

111   Gaetano Moroni (1802-1883), papal scholar and dignitary, authored, among other works, the *Dizionario di erudizione storico-ecclesiastica.*

112   Martorelli, vol. I, 425.

5.2   The Battle of Vienna (1683)

In 1683, one century after Lepanto, Christendom was once again in danger. Turkish expansionism was spreading in Europe, and it was once again the Roman Pontiff, at the time Innocent XI, who urged the Catholic States to take up arms to defend the Church and European civilization.

The decisive battle took place in Vienna, and here too, victory was obtained through the intercession of the Mother of God, venerated with the title of Virgin Lauretana. The victorious Christian army brought her image along as they entered the freed Austrian capital. The King of Poland, John Sobieski, and the Capuchin Father Marco D'Aviano, were the undisputed protagonists of that great Crusade against Islam.

In his already cited work *The Popes and the Holy House*, [113] Fr. Arsenio D'Ascoli, former director of the Universal Congregation, compellingly recalls the event:

"A century after their defeat at Lepanto (1571) the Turks tried to overcome Europe and Christianity by land. In early 1683, Mohammed IV gave the Banner of Muhammad to Kara Mustafa, making him swear to defend it unto death. The Grand Vizier, proud of his army of 300,000 soldiers, promised to overthrow Belgrade, Buda, Vienna, invade Italy all the way to Rome, and place the trough of his horse on the altar of St. Peter's.

"In August 1683, the Capuchin Father Marco D'Aviano was named Chief Chaplain of all the Christian armies. He revived the terrified people, and convinced John Sobieski to rush in with his 40,000-men army. The image of Our Lady was on every flag: Vienna confided only in her help. The city was besieged since July 14,

---

113   A. D'Ascoli, *I Papi e la Santa Casa*, Loreto, 1969, pp. 54 & ff.

and its surrender was a matter of hours. In a chapel on Kahlemberg Mountain, which overlooks the city from the north, Fr. Marco D'Aviano celebrated Mass with Sobieski as an acolyte, before the entire Christian army arranged in a semicircle. Father d'Aviano promised a most amazing victory. At the end of the Mass, as if in ecstasy, instead of saying: '*Ite Missa est*,' he shouted, '*Joannes vinces*,' that is: 'John, you will win.'

"The battle began at the dawn of September 11th. A splendid sun illuminated the two armies about to decide the fate of Europe. City bells rang apace, women and children were in church begging for Mary's help. Before the evening, the Turkish army fled, Muhammad's banner was in the hands of Sobieski, and the tent of Grand Vizier taken over. People eagerly flocked to contemplate the face of their hero. The following day, preceded by the great Banner of Muhammad, dressed in blue and gold, and mounted on the horse of the Grand Vizier, Sobieski made his solemn entry into the city amid delirious acclamations.

"On Sobieski's orders, the procession headed towards the church of Our Lady of Loreto, where a famous image of the Blessed Mother was venerated. The whole people gratefully prostrated at the feet of her to whom victory was owed. A Holy Mass was celebrated, attended by Sobieski, always on his knees as if absorbed in thought. The preacher climbed to the pulpit and gave a big speech of circumstance, applying to John Sobieski the words of the Gospel: '*Fuit homo missus a Deo cui nomen erat Joannes*' (there was a man sent from God, whose name was John).

"The simple ceremony went on with grandeur and solemnity, with picturesque details that highlighted Sobieski's faith and good spirits. The enemy siege had disorganized many things and the Church of Loreto no longer had singers. 'It doesn't matter,' said Sobieski, and at the foot of the altar, with his powerful voice, he led a *Te Deum*, which the people continued in unison. No organ or music was necessary, as the crowd chanted with piety, emotion, and enthusiasm. The baffled clergy did not know how to conclude and leafed through missals and rituals looking for a verse. Sobieski saved them from embarrassment; without paying much attention to the rubrics, he improvised, raising once again his still sonorous voice to the crowd: *'Non nobis, Domine, non nobis!'* ('Not to us, Lord, not to us!'). And the priests answered, shouting *'Sed nomini tuo da gloriam'* ('But to Thy Name give glory').

"Sobieski immediately sent a message to Blessed Innocent XI to announce the victory. The terms of the letter show the hero's humility and faith: *'Venimus, vidimus, et Deus vicit'* ('We have come, we have seen, and God has won'). A solemn embassy took to the Pope the great banner of Mohammed IV, the tent of the Grand Vizier, and a Christian flag retaken from the Turks. Grateful to Our Lady for that great victory, Blessed Innocent XI sent the flag taken from the Turks and the tent to her Shrine. The flag is still preserved in the Treasury Room. The tent was taken personally by Clementine, daughter of Sobieski and wife to James II King of England. With the tent, they made a precious canopy, used only in great solemnities. ... Like Sobieski, the Pope attributed the victory to Our Lady of Loreto. His ex-voto was to establish a feast in honor of the Most Holy Name of Mary. On November 25, 1683, an act of the Congregation of Rites extended it to the whole Church. St. Pius X set its celebration for September 12, the anniversary of the victory.

"After the great battle of Vienna, they found under the rubble a beautiful statue of Our Lady of Loreto, on the side of which was written: '*In hac imagine Mariae victor eris Joannes; In hac imagine Mariae vinces Joannes*'('John, with this image of Mary you will be victorious, John, with this image of Mary you will win'). It was certainly a statue brought there by Saint John of Capistrano over more than two centuries earlier, from in the battles against the Turks in Hungary and Belgrade.

"Sobieski had Fr. D'Aviano take it on the triumphal entry in Vienna the day after the victory. He had taken it with him when pursuing the enemy and achieved splendid victories against the Turks. He placed it in his chapel and had daily Mass celebrated in front of it, singing the Loreto Litanies. Prof. Gatti decided to recall this episode in the Polish Chapel of Loreto by placing on its right wall a picture Fr. Marco D'Aviano with Our Lady of Loreto in his hand. Blessed Innocent XI ordered a print of the Holy House with the inscription, 'Holy Mary of Loreto, pray for us,' on the 'Agnus Dei' of the first and seventh year of his pontificate."

In these, as in many other cases in history, Our Lady truly appeared "terrible as an army set in array" (Cant 6:10).

Outside the Polish chapel of the sanctuary, there is still a plaque explaining how Sobieski, after the battle, donated the loot taken from the Turks to the Loreto Sanctuary.

5.3 Heroic Defense of the Papal States

Two centuries later, another crusade was fought at the gates of Loreto, this time no longer against the Turks but against the liberal and Masonic revolution led

A century after Lepanto, in 1683, Christendom again found itself in danger. Turkish expansionism was rampant in Europe. The King of Poland, John Sobieski, and the Capuchin Father Marco d'Aviano were the undisputed protagonists of the great Crusade against Islam. Our Lady's image is on every flag. Arturo Gatti, 1912-1939. Polish chapel, Loreto Sanctuary

by the House of Savoy against the ancient Italian kingdoms and the Papal State.

On September 18, 1860, Christophe Léon-Louis Lamoricière, general of the papal army, valiantly fought to defend the Church in Castelfidardo, under the eyes of Our Lady, so to speak. During that battle, the head of the Papal Zouaves, Colonel George de Pimodan, heroically died after glancing at the Loreto sanctuary one last time.

"During the fight," one of the surviving volunteers later wrote, "I did not lose sight of the House of Loreto." Another soldier, turning to the Blessed Mother, said, "It is sweet to think, oh good Mother, that in five minutes a bullet will perhaps take me to you."

Eyewitnesses recount that all the Pope's soldiers, like true martyrs, "embraced suffering and death with the joy of the predestined; they lay on their blood as in a nuptial bed of immortal life, singing the songs of eternal love. At the feet of the Blessed Virgin, they found the holy heroism that animated them during the struggle; in the shadow of the Holy House, they came to offer to God, through Mary, the first fruits of their suffering, and some, their last sigh."[114]

Bishop Felix Dupanloup, in a funeral oration dedicated to those fallen for the Church and the Papacy, exclaimed, "Sanctuary of Loreto, they saw you as they fought! You appeared to them as a refuge open to their souls, and their dying eyes looked at you. These young people who came from Loreto full of life, returned there in the evening on stretchers, limbs mutilated, shouting in anguish. They prayed to their bearers to place them as close as possible to the divine mansion, and those who still had the strength dragged themselves on their hands and knees to approach and kiss its holy walls."[115]

114 A. Grillot, *La Sainte Maison de Lorette*, Alfred Mame et Fils Editeurs, Tours, 1876[7], Chap. XIII - I martiri di Castelfidardo, p. 169.

115 Cit. in G. Gorel, *La santa Casa di Loreto*, cit., p. 168.

Chapter VI

Where the Great Became Pilgrims

Other than saints, countless leading personalities of history visited the shrine of Loreto as pilgrims. Here too an exhaustive list would require a separate discussion,[116] so we will only give a few examples.

1) We must start with France, which has always had a special bond with the Holy House. As is known, the sanctuary houses several national chapels (Spanish, Polish, Swiss, German, Slavic, etc.), but the French one, dedicated to King St. Louis IX (1214-1270), has a special meaning.

The great sovereign went as a pilgrim to this holy abode when it was still in Nazareth. The visit took place on the eve of the Annunciation in 1251 after he was freed from the captivity of the Sultan of Egypt. The chapel and its paintings recall the episode and the crusade against the Mohammedans. On March 25, he received Holy Communion in the Holy House.

Here is how William of Nangis recounts that journey:

"As soon as he saw the city, he descended from his horse and adored Our Lord and venerated Our Lady. ... On that day, despite his labors, he fasted on bread and water. With how much devotion and solemnity he behaved, and with what splendor he had vespers, mass and other offices of this feast celebrated! All the numerous

---

116 See, about this matter, G. Santarelli, *Personaggi d'Autorità a Loreto*, Edizioni Santa Casa, Loreto 2010.

Two of the five red cloth crosses, insignia of Crusader pilgrims, found among the stones of the Holy House. They were discovered under the window during the archaeological excavations of the 1960s, and are preserved in the Historical Archives of the Sanctuary.

The Window of the Annunciation.

Nazareth.
Lithograph from the diary of David Roberts, 1842.

Ostrich egg found under the stones of the Holy House.

Coins of Guido II de la Roche, Duke of Athens (1287-1308), found in the basement of the Holy House.

(Left) St. Louis IX receives Communion in the Holy House of Nazareth. Carlos Lameire, 1896, French chapel

(Right) Saint Louis IX (1214-1270), King of France, went as a pilgrim to the holy abode when it was still in Nazareth, on the eve of the Annunciation in 1251, after being freed from the captivity of the Sultan of Egypt. In memory of this event and as a sign of thanksgiving and devotion, the king was depicted on the wall of the Holy House praying in front of an image of Our Lady. He is covered with the royal mantle and holds the fetters of his imprisonment in his right hand, and the scepter in his left.

people present can tell about it, and more than one will proclaim and testify that from the day the Son of God took his body from the Virgin Mary in this same place, never was he officially celebrated with so much solemnity and devotion. The pious King had the Mass sung 'in the place where the angel Gabriel greeted Our Lady.' At the end of the Mass, he received with great devotion and humility the true bread of angels, which is the true Body of Our Lord Jesus Christ. And then he returned to Jaffa."[117]

In remembrance of this event and as a sign of gratitude and devotion, the king is depicted on the wall of the Holy House in prayer in front of an image of Our Lady, covered with the royal mantle, and holding in his right hand the chains of his imprisonment, and on the left, his scepter. According to some, when the three

117 Cit. in G. Gorel, *La santa Casa*, cit., p. 34.

holy walls came to Trsat, the walls were already painted like that. The halo was evidently added later because Louis IX was canonized by Boniface VIII in 1297. Others claim that the fresco is from a later date. [118]

King Henry III of France (1551-1589), who was unable to have children, appealed to Our Lady of Loreto by sending to the Basilica a sapphire cup with a gold-set emerald foot. Its cover, made of rock crystal, supported a solid golden angel holding a diamond lily. [119]

Louis XIII (1601-1643), after 23 years of sterility of his wife Anne of Austria, by the grace of the Blessed Virgin of Loreto, finally succeeded in begetting the future Louis XIV (1638-1715). In thanksgiving, he gave a massive, 330-pound silver angel in the act of presenting to

---

118 Cf. G. Santarelli, *La Santa Casa di Loreto*, cit., p. 266; G. Gorel, *La santa Casa di Loreto*, cit., p. 35.

119 Cf. G. Gorel, *La santa Casa di Loreto*, cit., p. 157.

Mary a life-size child in gold weighing 24 pounds. Later, the Sun King asked and obtained that the feast of St. Louis IX be celebrated every August 25 in the Basilica, solemnly and in perpetuity. And in a letter of December 23, 1655, he asked the Pope to extend the feast of the miraculous translation of the Holy House to the universal Church on December 10.[120] That is why a French chaplain has been present in the sanctuary for centuries.

Princes, princesses, kings, and emperors became pilgrims in Loreto. Emperor Charles IV, John Palaeologus of Constantinople, Frederick III, Alfonso of Aragon, King of Naples, many Polish sovereigns, Emperor Charles V, Christian, King of Sweden, Archdukes Leopold, Ferdinand and Maximilian of Austria, Charles IV King of Spain, Queen Beatrice of Hungary, and the dukes of Savoy, Tuscany, Parma, Modena, and Mantua, to name just a few.

In 1598, Archduke Ferdinand, who later became Emperor Ferdinand II, went as a pilgrim to Loreto as a young man to promise to the Blessed Virgin that he would destroy the heresy spreading in Austria, even at the cost of his life. He did so and became a champion of the Counter-Reformation.

Also extraordinary was the assistance Our Lady gave the Hungarian Stephen V Báthory, one of the military glories of that country, in the Battle of Breadfield against the Turks on October 13, 1479. In desperate conditions, he managed to win after invoking the Most Holy Virgin of Loreto, and as a sign of appreciation, he gave the shrine a huge golden statue of the Virgin and Child.

2) The great poet Dante Alighieri, in his *Divine Comedy*, refers in passing to Loreto: "In that spot was

---

120 Cf. G. Gorel, *La santa Casa di Loreto*, cit., p. 211.

French chapel.

Pedro de Villa fulfills the vow in the Holy House on behalf of
Christopher Columbus's crew. Cesare Maccari, dome of the Basilica
of Loreto

I, Peter Damien / And Peter the sinner was in the House
/ Beside the Adriatic, in the house our blessed Lady"
(Paradise XXI), alluding to Saint Peter Damien, who
found himself in the Marche region well before the
translation, and to Saint Peter, who instead celebrated
Mass in the Holy House in Nazareth.

3) As can be read in his "Journal," Christopher Columbus knew the Loreto sanctuary very well and possi-
bly visited it as a young sailor when crossing the Adriatic between 1465 and 1475. On February 13, 1493,
while returning to Spain from the historic journey in
which he discovered the American continent, his fleet
was hit by a violent storm. The sea became very threatening and the wave tormented the two surviving ships,
the "Niña" and the "Pinta."

On the night of February 14, the wind intensified
further and the waves became appalling. The "Pinta" was
at the mercy of the wind, was taken off course, and disap-

The central nave of the Basilica of Loreto. On the south side of the cladding of the Holy House, there is the high altar, with the window of the Annunciation in the center

peared from sight. Faced with danger, Columbus and his sailors relied on the intercession of Our Lady, to whom they made three collective promises. As many chickpeas as were sailors on the "Niña" were put into a cap. One of the chickpeas was marked with a cross, and whoever extracted it would have to go on pilgrimage to three Marian shrines. The first and third draws fell on Columbus, who promised to go to the Spanish sanctuary of Santa Maria of Guadalupe in Extremadura, offering a five-pound

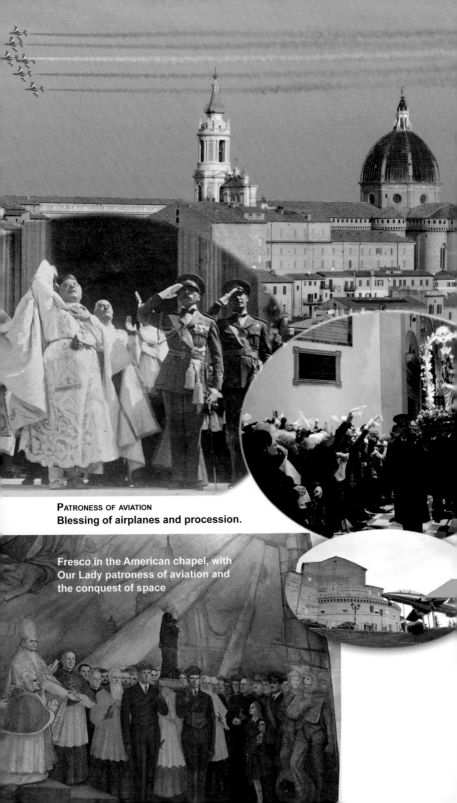

PATRONESS OF AVIATION
Blessing of airplanes and procession.

Fresco in the American chapel, with Our Lady patroness of aviation and the conquest of space

candle, and to that of Santa Clara di Moguer. The second drawing fell on a sailor, Pedro de Villa, to whom Columbus promised money to go "to Holy Mary of Loreto, located in the Mark of Ancona, in the Papal State, which is the House in which the Blessed Virgin has made and still makes many great miracles." After the three promises, the storm gradually subsided and the crew was finally able to land on the Spanish coast. In the dome of the Basilica of Loreto, the painter Cesare Maccari depicted Christopher Columbus fulfilling his vow.[121]

---

121 Cf. *Il voto di Cristoforo Colombo alla Madonna di Loreto*, in http://www.vivereosimo.it/2007/12/10/il-voto-di-cristoforo-colombo-alla-madonna-di-loreto/150119/.

The Polish military cemetery of the 2nd Army Corps, with the bodies of the soldiers who heroically gave their lives to take Loreto during the Second World War, is on the slope descending toward the plain and the sea.

4) Torquato Tasso dedicated some verses to the Holy House later taken up by the current Liturgy of the Hours for the feast day. When visiting the sanctuary as a pilgrim on October 31, 1587, he entrusted his sufferings and trials to Our Lady. In those years, he worked on a song titled *To the Most Blessed Virgin of Loreto.* Here are some verses:

Here the Angels raised the holy house,
That once received Mary with her holy Son;
They carried it over the clouds and above the water:
A great miracle, to which I lift up
My mind otherwise turned to the ground,
And oppressed by thoughts.
This is the Mount you deigned to honor
With your holy walls,
O Virgin chaste and pure;
Indeed your birth, and later, his own,
Made me envied by Mount Atlas;
For, despising its fabulous qualities,
You made me the humble stay of both the king
and royal family.

5) In Loreto lay the mortal remains of General Giuseppe La Hoz, one of the main protagonists of the anti-Jacobin insurrection of the Marche region during the era of the Napoleonic invasion. Born in Milan of Spanish origin, La Hoz initially supported Bonaparte and was a staunch advocate of Jacobinism. But he changed his mind and went over to Italian insurgents, leading the revolt in the Marche from June 17, 1799, and dying under the walls of Ancona at the end of September 1799. He entered Loreto on August 4 of the same year, and the French definitively abandoned the Marian city, which fell under the imperial-royal pontifical Regency, established on the preceding July 11 for the Mark of Ancona and Fermo.

Monaldo Leopardi, in his *Autobiography*, writes that he believes "for certain that La Hoz had the genius and thoughts of Bonaparte and only circumstances made them unlike." However, the fact is that the day after his death, the body of the general was taken to the Basilica of Loreto and buried with great honors in its cemetery crypt, now called Crypt of the Crucifix. Exhumations in 1941 and 1995 found his body still well preserved.[122]

6) The great counter-revolutionary journalist Louis Veuillot confirmed his devotion to the Holy House in his work *Rome and Loreto* (1841): "It will never occur to us that God would deceive our piety and love. Had He not ordered his angels to take this house that was the theater of the first mystery of our salvation, to the heart of the Catholic world, He would certainly have been able to make any fallacious imitation of it disappear. And just as He could easily annihilate a vain imitation, He could just as easily offer to our veneration these holy stones, which, according to His august designs, should be torn from the hands of infidels. ... There is no place for error when God intervenes with sensational and miraculous gestures to support something He wants to make known with certainty. Everyone knows the unquestionable truth that Providence, supremely wise, would not employ supernatural testimonies of its power to induce men into error. Now [in this case], supernatural testimonies, otherwise called miracles, are innumerable."

---

122 Cf. *Il Messaggio della Santa Casa*, no. 8, September-October 2015.

Loreto, the Sanctuary of "Non-negotiable Principles"

Loreto is a sanctuary that can serve as a spiritual "lung," especially for those who struggle to defend non-negotiable principles (right to life, defense of the natural family, right of parents to educate their children).

The events that took place in the Holy House, of really great importance for the history of humanity, and all the more for those who profess the Christian religion, leave no room for doubt.[123]

• Defending the right to life from conception...

Our Redemption began among those sacred walls. Not only was Our Lord Jesus Christ conceived there; it was also the place of Mary's Immaculate Conception and birth. Within those walls, the Word became flesh and came to dwell among men. How can we not then think of the intrinsic dignity of human beings from the moment of conception? Jesus himself, the Savior, assumed the human condition right from the beginning. Our Lord was an embryo and a fetus and lived for nine months in the virginal womb of Mary Most Holy.

• ... to natural death

Let us not forget that, according to tradition, St. Joseph died in the Holy House of Nazareth, assisted by

---

123 Cf. Benedict XVI, *Discorso ai partecipanti al convegno promosso dal Partito Popolare Europeo*, March 30, 2006, in https://w2.vatican.va/content/benedict-xvi/it/speeches/2006/march/documents/hf_ben-xvi_spe_20060330_eu-parliamentarians.html.

Mary Most Holy and by Our Lord. For this reason, the glorious patriarch became the patron saint of the dying. No one in the world had such great grace—passing from this life to the next in the arms of Our Lady and Jesus. St. Joseph's was a blessed death, crowning a life entirely spent at the service of God, of whom he voluntarily made himself a docile instrument.

Well then, for Catholics, Loreto can become the spiritual point of reference for the struggle against any legislation aiming to introduce euthanasia, often disguised with expressions such as "assisted suicide" or living will (in the name of false mercy). Attacks on life in its terminal phase are very dangerous because they seek to recognize only viable and healthy lives as having human dignity. But human beings always preserve their nobility in every condition and situation, no matter how painful and tragic it may be. The sick need to not be killed, but rather assisted by their loved ones and receive care that alleviates suffering, just as happened with St. Joseph. Eliminating the sick is not a gesture of love but selfishness, which hides many economic interests and above all the agenda of the "culture of death."

- **Defense of the Natural Family,
  Founded on Marriage and Private Property**

The Holy House of Nazareth is the place where the Holy Family, the model of all families, lived. Therefore, Loreto is the privileged place to pray for the institution of the family, now threatened inside and outside the Church. Today we must engage the decisive battle, both in the temporal and spiritual spheres, to defend the indissolubility of marriage and the only true family, composed of a man and a woman. Facing the rising tide of dominant fashions, the Holy House of Loreto must become the center from which one should draw strength to reaffirm a clear "No" to divorce, to out-of-wedlock cohabitation, feminism, transgenderism, and homosexual unions, sins that destroy the fundamental building block of society, which is a stable and united family. And considering that the Holy Family owned the Holy House, one must fight for true social justice, which requires the recognition and protection of the right of private property, with a consequent family-friendly economy that supports the birth rate.

- **Primordial Right of Parents to Educate their Offspring**

In the Holy House, Our Lord Jesus Christ grew and was educated by his Mother and by St. Joseph. Jesus lived with his parents up to the age of thirty, a whole existence made of prayer and work, obedience and sacrifice, sobriety and purity. Among those walls, Our Lady herself was raised and educated by her parents, Joachim and Anna. Loreto is, therefore, the point of reference also on this topic, so trampled upon today. Faced with state-controlled secular public schools that instill religious indifferentism and anti-Christian values, and the imposition of gender ideology, which aims to dissolve human nature itself, it is more necessary than ever to reiterate the primordial right of parents to educate their children based on the principles they believe in. Hence, there is also a need to create authentically Catholic parental schools free from state constraints. No power may snatch children from their families and indoctrinate them against the will of their parents.

- **The Struggle for Purity and Chastity**

The Holy House welcomed a special, entirely holy family characterized by perpetual virginity. Jesus, Mary, and Joseph preserved integral purity and chastity throughout their lives, in body and spirit. For many people today, even Catholics, living in continence before marriage, during the marriage, or throughout life seems an impossible undertaking. Meanwhile, pornography has become as rampant and unrestrained as contraception. People have lost the sense of sacrifice and purity to the point that every whim and pleasure seems to have to become a legally recognized, protected, and even required right. Conversely, the Holy Family lived in complete purity as a single great offering to God, truly becoming an example for everyone – children, young people, adults, and elderly – today increasingly crushed by the all-pervasive sexual revolution.

"Porta Marina" (Marine Gate). Wall of Loreto, seventeenth-century

"Porta Marina" (*Marine Gate*). Wall of Loreto, seventeenth-century door that opens behind the apses of the Sanctuary

BIBLIOGRAPHY

Books and Journals

ANNALI della Santa Casa di Loreto, monthly journal, Year XXVI, no.2, February 1923.

APOLLONIO A.M., *Le Litanie Lauretane*, Casa Mariana Editrice, Frigento (AV), 2013.

BARGILESI N., *Trattato utile sopra la vera et sincera historia della santa chiesa et Casa della gloriosa Vergine Maria di Loreto*, Edizione Francesco Rampazetto, Venezia, 1566.

BARTOLI B., *Le glorie maestose del Santuario di Loreto*, in Macerata, 1696.

BERNARDO Saint, *Omelie sulla Madonna,* Opera omnia, ed. Cisterc. 4, 1966.

BLASI R., *Studio critico sulla S. Casa Lauretana*, Unione Cattolica Tipografica, Macerata, 1906.

CAILLAUX A.R., *Histoire critique et religieuse de Notre Dame de Lorette*, Paris, 1843.

CAVATORTI Fr., *Le guarigioni a Loreto. Gli sguardi e le carezze della Madonna*, Congregazione Universale della Santa Casa, Loreto, 2001.

D'ANGHIARI A, & Vv.Aa., *Il Santuario di Loreto*, Congregazione Universale della Santa Casa, Loreto, 1957.

D'ASCOLI A., *La Santa Casa*, Congregazione Universale della Santa Casa, 1965.

D'ASCOLI A., *I Papi e la Santa Casa*, Congregazione Universale della Santa Casa, Loreto, 1969.

DELLA CASA R., *Memoria storiche documentate sulla Santa Casa di Loreto*, Tip. San Bernardino, Siena, 1909.

GAUDENTI A., *Storia della Santa Casa di Loreto esposta in dieci brevi ragionamenti fra un sacerdote custode di S. Casa ed un divoto pellegrino*, Congregazione Universale della Santa Casa, Loreto, 1790.

GOREL G., *La santa Casa di Loreto*, Edizioni Paoline, Catania, 1962.

GRILLOT A., *La Sainte Maison de Lorette*, Alfred Mame et Fils Editeurs, Tours, 1876.

IL MESSAGGIO DELLA SANTA CASA, no.7, July-August 2000, 80° Anniversario della proclamazione della Madonna di Loreto a Patrona dell'Aviazione.

IL MESSAGGIO DELLA SANTA CASA, n. 8, September-October 2015.

IL MESSAGGIO DELLA SANTA CASA, n. 7, July-August 2017.

L'ECO DELLA S. CASA DI LORETO, monthly journal, Year I, no.1, May 1881.

L'ECO DELLA S. CASA DI LORETO, monthly journal, Year II, no.16, August 1882.

MARTORELLI P.V., *Teatro istorico della Santa Casa*, Roma 1732-1735.

MONELLI N., *La Santa Casa a Loreto-La Santa Casa a Nazareth*, Edizioni Santa Casa, Loreto, 1997.

MONELLI N. – Santarelli G., *L'altare degli Apostoli nella Santa Casa di Loreto*, Edizioni Santa Casa, Loreto, 2012.

MONTANARI M. – Schiaroli A., *Santi e beati a Loreto*, Congregazione Universale Santa Casa, Loreto, 2005.

MURRI V., *Dissertazione critico-istorica sulla identità della Santa Casa di Nazarette ora venerata in Loreto*, Edizioni Carnevali, Loreto, 1791.

NICOLINI G., *La veridicità storica della Miracolosa Traslazione della Santa Casa di Nazareth a Loreto*, Ed. Tele Maria, Ancona, 2004.

NICOLINI G., in *Nuovi studi confermano l'autenticità della Santa Casa di Maria a Loreto*, Agenzia Internazionale Zenit, Roma, 28 marzo 2006.

NICOLINI G., "L'approvazione dei Sommi Pontefici delle miracolose traslazioni della Santa Casa di Nazareth a Loreto," in *Il Segno del soprannaturale*, no. 209, November 2005.

NICOLINI G., "Le 'prove' delle miracolose traslazioni dalle rivelazioni mistiche di Santa Caterina da Bologna e della Beata Caterina Emmerich," in *Il Segno del soprannaturale*, no.208, October 2005.

NICOLINI G., "Alcune 'prove' storiche, archeologiche e scientifiche comprovanti 'la verità' delle miracolose traslazioni della Santa Casa di Nazareth a Loreto," in *Il Segno del soprannaturale* no. 210, December 2005.

NICOLINI G., "Le cinque traslazioni 'miracolose' della Santa Casa di Nazareth, in Il segno del soprannaturale," no. 215, May 2006.

NICOLINI G., "Le cinque traslazioni 'miracolose' della Santa Casa di Nazareth, storicamente documentate," in *Il segno del soprannaturale*, no. 220, October 2006.

NICOLINI G., "Le cinque traslazioni 'miracolose' della Santa Casa di Nazareth," in *Il segno del soprannaturale*, no. 222, December 2006.

PACE G.M., *Miracolosa Traslazione a Loreto della dimora della Santissima Annunziata*, Priorato Madonna di Loreto, Rimini.

REY-MERMET T., *Il santo del secolo dei lumi*, Città Nuova, Firenze, 1983.

RICCARDI A., *Storia apologetica della Santa Casa di Nazzaret a Loreto*, stamperia Mazzoleni, Bergamo, 1842.

RIERA R., *Historia Domus Lauretanae Liber singularis*, 1565.

SANTARELLI G., *I graffiti della Santa Casa di Loreto,* Edizioni Santa Casa, Loreto, 2010.

SANTARELLI G., *Personaggi d'Autorità a Loreto,* Edizioni Santa Casa, Loreto, 2010.

SINIBALDI R., *Cronichetta della Prodigiosa Traslazione della S. Casa di Maria Vergine di Nazareth*, Fratelli Rossi, Loreto, 1844.

SANTARELLI G., *La Santa Casa di Loreto*, Edizioni Santa Casa, Loreto 2014,

TORSELLINI O., *Lauretanae Historiae libri quinque*, Rome, 1597.

TROMBELLI B., *Translatio Almae Domus Lauretanae*, Typis Chiappini et Cortesi, Macerata, 1783.

VUILLAUME G.B., *La S. Casa di Loreto, Prove autentiche del Miracolo della Traslazione*, Rome, 1884.

Sites and links

BENEDICT XVI, Pastoral Visit to Loreto on the Agorà meeting of Italian youth (September 1-2 settembre, 2007) in https://w2.vatican.va/content/benedict-xvi/it/travels/2007/inside/documents/loreto.html

BENEDICT XVI, Homily during the pastoral visit to Loreto on the 50th anniversary of the trip of John XXIII, in https://w2.vatican.va/content/benedict-xvi/it/homilies/2012/documents/hf_ben-xvi_hom_20121004_loreto.html

PAPAL DELEGATION Holy House of Loreto, www.santuarioloreto.it

JOHN PAUL II, Letter to Msgr. Pasquale Macchi on the VII centenary of the translation of the Holy House of Loreto, August 15, 1993 in: https://w2.vatican.va/content/john-paul-ii/it/letters/1993/documents/hf_jp-ii_let_19930815_mons-macchi.html

NICOLINI G., *La Voce Cattolica*, sez. Santa Casa, in: www.lavocecattolica.it/santacasa.htm

NICOLINI G., Tele Maria, sez. video "Santa Casa", in: www.telemaria.it

NICOLINI G., History Archive of the Weekly Newsletter *Notiziario di TeleMaria/LaVoceCattolica*, in: http://d9i1c.s76.it/frontend/nl_catalog.aspx

PIUS XII, Radiomessage to participants of the national pilgrimage to the Sanctuary of the Blessed Virgin Mary of Loreto, October 14, 1956, in https://w2.vatican.va/content/pius-xii/it/speeches/1956/documents/hf_p-xii_spe_19561014_pellegrinaggio-loreto.html

PIUS XII, Speech to the faithful of the Marche region residing in Rome, March 23, 1958, in https://w2.vatican.va/content/pius-xii/it/speeches/1958/documents/hf_p-xii_spe_19580323_marchigiani.html

The Miracle of the
HOLY HOUSE OF LORETO

In the hill country of central Italy, on the Musone River just south of Ancona and near the Adriatic coast, lies the town of Loreto. This humble place has the immense privilege of hosting one of the most important relics of Christianity: the Holy House of the Blessed Virgin Mary. In fact, here are preserved the three walls within which God became man and our Redemption began. In that dwelling, Our Lady was conceived, born and received the announcement of the Archangel Gabriel. She also lived there with Jesus and her husband, Saint Joseph.

The Shrine of Loreto, as Pope John Paul II wrote, is the "first sanctuary of international importance dedicated to the Virgin Mary and, for several centuries, the true Marian heart of Christianity."

It is also a perpetual miracle, which still raises questions and curiosity. How can one prove that the three walls are indeed those of the Holy Family's House? How did they come from Nazareth to Italy? Was it the work of angels or crusaders? Did the House come directly to Loreto or did it stop in other locations? What about the importance of the Holy House, or Casa Sancta, in the struggle between Christendom and Islam? What miracles have occurred in connection with the Holy House of Loreto, and which saints and famous people have visited it?

This book will answer these questions and highlight this treasure chest of history, faith and tradition, which Italy has the grace to preserve.